POOP HAPPENED!

A HISTORY OF THE WORLD FROM THE BOTTOM UP

SARAH ALBEE

illustrated by **ROBERT LEIGHTON**

Walker & Company
New York

For Georgie,
who taught me to examine
the human condition
from the bottom up
—S. A.

For Sammy and Sophie
—R. L.

Text copyright © 2010 by Sarah Albee
Illustrations copyright © 2010 by Robert Leighton

First published in the United States of America in May 2010
by Walker Publishing Company, Inc., a division of Bloomsbury Publishing, Inc.
www.bloomsburykids.com

For information about permission to reproduce selections from this book, write to
Permissions, Walker BFYR, 175 Fifth Avenue, New York, New York 10010

Library of Congress Cataloging-in-Publication Data
Albee, Sarah.
Poop happened! : a history of the world from the bottom up / by Sarah Albee ;
illustrated by Robert Leighton. — 1st U.S. ed.
p.   cm.
ISBN 978-0-8027-2077-1 (paperback) • ISBN 978-0-8027-9825-1 (reinforced)
1. Toilets—History—Juvenile literature. 2. Toilets—Great Britain—History—Juvenile literature.
I. Leighton, Robert, ill. II. Title.
GT476.A54 2010   363.72'88—dc22   2009034172

Printed in China by Leo Paper Products, Heshan, Guangdong
4 6 8 10 9 7 5 3 (paperback)
2 4 6 8 10 9 7 5 3 (reinforced)

All papers used by Bloomsbury Publishing, Inc., are natural, recyclable products
made from wood grown in well-managed forests. The manufacturing processes
conform to the environmental regulations of the country of origin.

Contents

Preface

WELCOME TO THE PREFACE. This is the place where I explain to you my reasons for writing this book. Because you may be wondering, why a whole book about the history of poop?

Personally, I was tired of *not* reading about poop. Most history books just don't talk about it, but they should. Poop is important, and we can't afford to ignore it. Eliminating waste is something every living thing does. Figuring out how to deal with poop has been an issue ever since people started living in groups, and it's *still* an issue.

Okay, I also happen to think toilet humor is funny. I used to scold my kids when they used potty talk, but secretly, I was trying not to crack up.

I should tell you right now that I am not a real historian. I'm a children's book writer, which really is the world's funnest job. But I have always been *interested* in history. When I was a kid, I actually liked going on field trips and even visiting museums (especially if they contained things like torture instruments and gory paintings). But the part about studying history that drove me smack out of my mind was having to learn about kings and queens and battles and dates, and having to look at pictures that showed rich people in fancy clothes. I didn't so much care who Queen So-and-so married; I wanted to know how she fit through a doorway wearing that skirt. I wasn't interested in when General So-and-so fought a certain battle; I wanted to know how he could sit down in those tight breeches.

What I realize now is that I had no real connection to the people I saw in those images and read about in those books. I was much more interested in learning about how ordinary people lived. What did they wear? How did they get around? What did their homes look like? What did they eat? And, most urgent of all for me, how did they go to the bathroom? So I decided to concentrate on that last question, and I set out to find as much information as I could.

Conveniently enough, I *married* a historian. After quite a few years of marriage, I began to notice there were a lot of history books lying around the house, and from time to time I would pick one up and read it. And I discovered that history books have changed a lot since I was a kid. They now include more information about how ordinary people lived their lives. Still, if you ask me, there's not enough about how people went to the bathroom.

Now, as I previously noted, despite what your parents and teachers may tell you, toilet talk *is* funny. And I can't be the first to have noticed this, but what you read in history books tends *not* to be funny. Just when you think to yourself, as you're reading along in your textbook, there's no way people can be more horrible to one another than *that,* you go on to read about some other horrible thing people did to one another that was even worse. Frankly, I don't know how my husband gets out of bed in the morning, having to teach these terrible things to high school kids each and every day. But if, like me, you're the sort who likes to look on the lighter side of things, then this book is for you. Because learning about how people coped with poop is not only a good way to learn a little bit about history, it can be funny too. Not always, mind you. (There aren't too many thigh-slapping moments in the cholera chapter, for instance.) But where it isn't amusing, at least it's disgusting, which can be nearly as fun.

But I want to apologize to you for something. I'm sorry that this book turned out to be so centered on the Western Hemisphere. I didn't intend for this to happen. It's just how it worked out. I was limited by two things: first, people from other parts of the world may have had interesting bathroom customs, but chroniclers of their time tended not to write about these customs very often. Perhaps they were under the impression that such things weren't worthy or interesting enough to preserve for posterity. Which is a real pity.

Second, there's the language barrier—whenever someone did decide to record some toileting facts in these remote (to us) parts of the world, odds are their accounts didn't get translated into English. It's difficult enough to uncover facts about how people from European and American societies went to the bathroom, let alone find translations of accounts from other parts of the world. I found a few, but I wish I'd found more.

What little I did find out indicated to me that in the pretoilet era, people confronted the same kinds of problems all over the world. I've focused a lot on London because that's where the toilet was invented, and what happened there in the nineteenth century is happening in urban areas in developing countries all over the world today—overcrowding, poor sanitation, even cholera outbreaks. And because the Victorians loved keeping statistics and cataloging details, it was relatively easy to uncover information about that time and place. But again, sorry about the Eurocentricity thing.

I used a lot of secondary sources to research this book. I relied on the accounts of real historians, scientists, and medical practitioners who have thoroughly researched specific places, subjects, and time periods. Then I sorted out what they had to say about sanitation and personal hygiene and assembled all that information. I also relied on several history-of-toilets books aimed at grown-ups, and I incorporated many of the details from those books into a broader historical context so you could see how sanitation fits into the great sweep of history. I owe a huge debt to all these writers, and I hope you will check them out in the endnotes and do further reading and Web surfing if you find a subject or time period that especially interests you.

Thanks for slogging all the way through this preface. I hope you find the book entertaining and informative. I can tell you that writing it was really fun, but I think that my family and friends are all very happy I've finally finished the book.

The Cradle
of Civilization

· 1 ·
Poop Matters

SALUTE YOUR TOILET

TAKE A GOOD LOOK at your toilet. Have you ever really thought about how it works? It may not look like much, but it's an engineering marvel.

The bathroom is a place you go roughly six times a day, whether it's to use the toilet, take a shower or bath, or wash your hands and face. So next time you're in there, watch the water swirl down the drain or the toilet bowl. Notice how easy it is to turn your faucet on and off, and how quickly the water that comes out of it warms up or cools down. Then ask yourself, If I had to choose, which would I rather live without: my computer or my toilet?

Practically everyone has heard of Thomas Edison, inventor of the electric lightbulb. But who's ever heard of Alexander Cummings, inventor of the modern flush toilet? Well, now *you* have.

In this book we're going to explore human history from a unique angle, starting with the dawn of civilization and moving toward the present day. We're going to look at how people have dealt with this most basic human function—eliminating waste from the body. We're going to examine people's daily lives, some of the especially disgusting jobs they performed, where they went to answer "nature's call," how sanitary their homes and streets were, what they wore and how clothing affected the design of their toilets, and, most important, why disposing of waste was—and still is—such a vital issue to their very survival, whether they knew it or not.

IT'S RAINING MEN

The year is 1618, the place, Bohemia. An angry mob of Protestant rebels is marching through the streets of Prague. Armed and dangerous, they cross the courtyard of Prague's main castle and storm up the stairs of the tower, where four Catholic ministers, councilors to the king, are discussing the crisis. The mob crams into the small room. The terrified ministers flatten themselves against the wall, begging to be allowed to leave. Two of them are released. The other two remain, along with their servant.

Then someone in the crowd has an idea. "Throw them out the window!" he yells.

The mob cheers with enthusiastic agreement. One at a time, the ministers are hauled to the sill and shoved out of the window, fifty feet above the ground, followed by their unlucky servant.

This event, which became known as the Defenestration of Prague, was an open act of defiance against the king. It marked the beginning of the bloody and pointless Thirty Years' War, during which quite a few noblemen and thousands and thousands of peasants died. By the end of the war, no one actually remembered why they had been fighting in the first place, and things returned more or less to the way they had been before.

But here's the part most textbooks leave out: Those councilors and their servant did not die from the fall. All three of them survived. Why?

Because they landed in a huge pile of poop.

It was heaped beneath the tower window. We're not talking about pigeon droppings here, or even one deposit from a passing horse. Imagine what a sizable mound it would have had to have been in order to cushion a fifty-foot fall.

Now, wouldn't you like to know what the poop was doing there?

WHY SHOULD WE CARE ABOUT THE HISTORY OF POOP?

LEARNING ABOUT HOW PEOPLE from different periods of history dealt with evacuating and then disposing of their own waste isn't just disgusting and—come on, admit it—interesting, it's an essential part of the history of human civilization.

As you read further in this book and learn more about how cities developed, you may find yourself arriving at a startling realization. In fact, we'll save you some trouble and get to the point right now: throughout human history, the most successful civilizations have been those that paid attention to plumbing.

Or, if you're one who tends to look at things from the darker side, we can summarize it for you this way: throughout history, the improper disposal of human waste has led to very bad consequences, namely, wars, disease, grisly deaths, insect trouble, plagues, high infant mortality, heavy alcohol consumption, shortened stature, shortened life spans, cave-ins, explosions, asphyxiation, peasant revolts, and collapsed empires.

To say nothing of extremely smelly city streets.

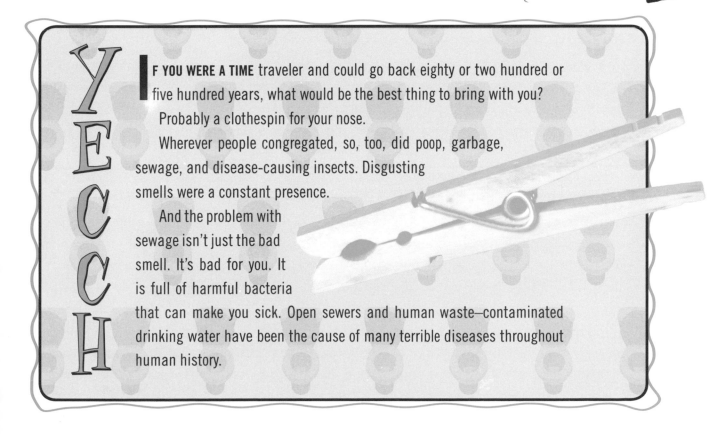

Y E C C H

IF YOU WERE A TIME traveler and could go back eighty or two hundred or five hundred years, what would be the best thing to bring with you?

Probably a clothespin for your nose.

Wherever people congregated, so, too, did poop, garbage, sewage, and disease-causing insects. Disgusting smells were a constant presence.

And the problem with sewage isn't just the bad smell. It's bad for you. It is full of harmful bacteria that can make you sick. Open sewers and human waste—contaminated drinking water have been the cause of many terrible diseases throughout human history.

WHAT TEXTBOOKS DON'T TELL YOU

And did he leave the lid up or down?

HOW DID A KNIGHT wearing fifty pounds of armor go to the bathroom? How did an eighteenth-century French countess fit through a bathroom doorway when wearing a skirt as wide as your teacher's desk? Why was there a huge pile of poop beneath the window of that tower in Bohemia? (See page 6.)

Textbooks don't tell you this stuff. In fact, they leave out a *lot* of information that the average kid really wants to know. They are full of facts about battles and treaties and rulers, but odds are, if you thumbed through them in search of information about bathrooms, you'd be wasting your time.

THE REAL POOP ON THE INDUSTRIAL REVOLUTION

WHENEVER PEOPLE PACK CLOSELY together and form a village or a town or a city, they need a reliable source of food to sustain them. Back in the Middle Ages, before there were superhighways and big trucks, the size of a town was limited by how much food could be grown on the surrounding farmland. Farmers carted food into town. In turn, waste from the town's residents got carted out and was either dumped into the nearest body of water or churned into the soil as fertilizer.

By the middle of the nineteenth century, with the arrival of trains and better roads, food could be carted in from farms that were much farther away. As a result, the populations of cities were able to grow a lot bigger, and in many places, populations exploded. For instance, by the late 1800s, London suddenly had three million people packed inside about 76 square miles—and we won't even talk about how many horses there were. (Actually, we will, but not until page 105, "Crossing Sweeper" box.) This period in history is known as the Industrial Revolution.

Frantic city planners scrambled to figure out what to do. With so many people moving in so rapidly, and packing together more closely than at any time in history, probably the most urgent and perplexing issue on everyone's mind was, *Where are we going to put all this poop?*

EVERYONE POOPS

ONE PROBLEM WITH STUDYING the past is that the people who would have the most interesting and relevant things to say about it are all dead. So the only information we have to go on comes from things they left behind—hieroglyphics, artifacts, pictures on urns, illuminated manuscripts, paintings, letters, and diaries. But most of these items tell us only about the lives of dead *rich* people.

It's usually relatively easy to uncover information about rich and famous people who lived a long time ago. Wealthy people kept diaries and wrote letters or even had others write books about them. Most scribes and pottery makers and fresco painters from days gone by were strongly encouraged (possibly on pain of death) to focus their artistic attention upon their wealthy employers.

But statistically speaking, your ancestors were probably not members of the elite ruling class. They were much more likely to have had to work for a living. After all, *96 percent of the people who have ever lived have been laborers.* Most of them spent their lives toiling away at life-shortening, mind-numbing jobs so that the wealthy 4 percent could eat well, keep warm, and enjoy themselves.

To make things even harder for historians interested in ordinary people, most members of this laboring class couldn't read or write. And

All work and no play— EVER.

even if they could, and could afford to buy paper and a pen, they would have been too busy struggling to survive to record much about their lives. So, very little information exists about 96 percent of the people who have ever lived.

But the great thing about studying people's bathroom habits is that it allows you to learn all kinds of fascinating, um, "dirt" about how all kinds of people lived—from the loftiest king to the lowliest sewer hunter. You'll be amazed at the sorts of things we can find out. You will also come to appreciate the many plumbers whose names have been lost to history but who, collectively, advanced civilization as much as any king or general or philosopher—because, after all, everyone has to go.

FLUSHED WITH (FALSE) PRIDE

The first patents for flushing toilets were filed about two hundred years ago. But as recently as a hundred and fifty years ago, most homes still had no toilets. The new toilets were so pricey, only wealthy people could afford to install them.

Although at first they were considered status symbols, the early toilets didn't work very well. They smelled, they leaked, and the noise they made when they flushed was deafening. And because they were not hooked up to sewer lines (which didn't exist), they often flooded people's basements or yards.

So chances are, if you lived in a town or a city any time in history up until about 1850, you were pretty much on your own when it came to disposing of the poop, garbage, and other waste products that were generated by the people in your household.

It wasn't until cities started building decent sewers that flush toilets had any chance of functioning properly—and most cities didn't get around to it until the late part of the nineteenth century. As sewer systems were built, the incidence of many diseases dropped significantly. Coincidence? Keep reading.

DON'T POOH-POOH THE POWER OF POOP

EVER SINCE THE DAWN of human civilization, access to clean water has been a matter of life and death. Those of us who enjoy decent plumbing are cleaner, are healthier, and live longer than ever before in history. But human poop, when improperly disposed of, can be a highly toxic substance. If it enters the drinking water, it can even become a weapon of mass destruction. More than a billion people today are forced to use polluted water for cooking, drinking, and bathing. And millions still die of poop-transmitted diseases.

The invention of the mass-produced, relatively inexpensive flushing toilet is one of the best things that ever happened to civilization. But it's important to realize that toilets are also responsible for a lot of problems, which we'll encounter later in this book.

Still, when you compare your life now to what life must have been like before toilets, you should thank your lucky stars you were born in a post-toilet era.

Like the inhabitants in this Brazilian favela, more than a third of the world's population—2.6 billion people—still has no decent place to go to the bathroom.

· 2 ·
Bad Plumbing?
Bad News

THE SCOOP ON HUMAN POOP

AWFUL DISEASES HAVE AFFLICTED humans ever since our ancestors lived in caves. And many of these diseases are the result of people accidentally swallowing water that contains tiny particles of other people's waste. Poop contains pathogens—organisms that cause disease—like bacteria, viruses, and parasites. At least fifty known diseases can be transferred from one person to another by way of contaminated poop.

Of the four ways you can catch a germ—through the air, through the water, by touch, or by getting bitten by an insect—three can be blamed on bad plumbing. (See box on "Some Poop-Related Poxes," pages 16–17.)

Leaky pipes, faulty faucets, and crumbling sewers spell disaster when the sewage seeps into people's drinking water. But for thousands of years, people didn't understand the link. They dumped their waste into the nearest river, then dipped their buckets back into that same water and drank it. Many wore just one set of very smelly clothes and lived under the same roof as their livestock, which resulted in swarms of disease-carrying insects crawling around inside their homes and all over their bodies.

Over the course of history these diseases have killed millions of people. The big three—cholera, typhoid, and dysentery—have killed a lot more soldiers during wartime than guns have.

Time and again, empires collapsed because they got pummeled by plagues and poxes. Sure, invading bloodthirsty barbarians may have helped things along. But disease was what ultimately did them in. The fall of Athens, the ruin of Rome, the collapse of the Byzantine Empire—all can be attributed, at least in part, to the fact that droves of people

living too close together contracted and died of horrifically contagious diseases.

And in spite of amazing advances in medicine and public health, many of these diseases continue to kill people today. In countries with contaminated drinking water and bad sewage systems, diarrhea is a terrible killer.

PRE-TOILET TOILET TERMS

aqueduct: A pipe or channel that relies on gravity to deliver water, sometimes over long distances.

cesspit: Also referred to as a cesspool, the cesspit is a place where sewage and other household garbage is collected. Cesspits must be emptied, as they don't drain into anything.

chamber pot: A pot into which you urinate (pee) or defecate (poop).

cistern: A container that usually holds rainwater or stored drinking water. Ancient flush toilets often relied on cisterns and gravity to flush away waste.

closestool: A box with a lid that encloses a chamber pot. The closestool dates back to the Renaissance. It is also sometimes called a commode, a night stool, or, in France, a *chaise percée.*

garderobe: A medieval latrine that was built into the wall of a castle. Waste fell into the moat below, or down a chute.

midden heap: A dung heap; a place where waste is deposited.

outhouse: Generally an American term (the English say "privy"), it's a building, separate from a house, that contains one or more seats placed over a cesspit.

privy: Also called a privy pit, necessary, bog house . . . there are hundreds of nicknames, but they're all terms for some sort of nonflushable latrine situated over a cesspit.

water closet (or WC): Nowadays, it's another name for the bathroom (a place with a flushing toilet), but since ancient times, it referred to a room in which water flushed away waste, either by gravity or by actual workable plumbing parts.

DISEASES CAUSED BY BUGS

THE MOST DANGEROUS THREATS to humans over the course of history have not been saber-toothed tigers or boats full of Vikings or even armies wielding guns and bombs. Ironically, the enemies that have been most successful at reducing human populations have been tiny insects.

Insects do more than annoy us. They cause disease, either directly or indirectly. Of the ten plagues of Egypt mentioned in the Old Testament, seven are linked to either bugs, bad sanitation, or both.

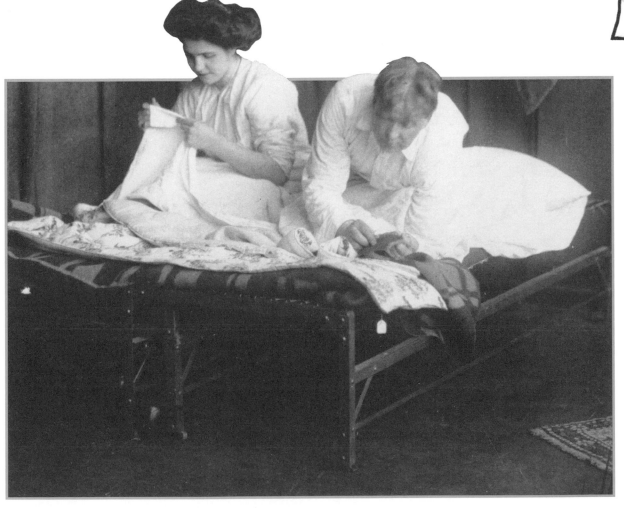

Creepy-crawly things have shared people's beds for centuries.

SOME POOP-RELATED POXES, PLAGUES, AND OTHER DISMAL DISEASES

Cholera (KAH-ler-uh): It's a doozy of a disease—painful, horrifying to witness, and highly contagious. It infects its victims when they drink contaminated water. The virus attacks the intestines, resulting in violent vomiting and diarrhea. It can kill a person in twelve hours, and all the gruesome stuff expelled by the victim can easily infect other people. (See chapter 13 for more on cholera.)

Dysentery (DIS-en-ter-ee), **giardia** (jee-AR-dee-a), **cryptosporidiosis** (KRIP-toe-spo-rid-ee-OH-sis): All diseases characterized by violent and painful diarrhea. You can catch them by drinking or swimming in polluted water or by touching a germy surface.

Escherichia coli (esh-a-RIK-ee-a KOH-lie): Usually abbreviated as E. coli, this is a leading cause of food-borne illness. People who get infected with a bad strain of E. coli suffer from bloody diarrhea, which can occasionally lead to kidney failure and even death. You catch it by eating undercooked ground beef or other contaminated foods, such as leafy vegetables, or by swimming in or drinking sewage-contaminated water.

Polio (POH-lee-oh): Poliomyelitis, as it is technically known, is a virus that can sometimes attack the spinal cord and cause paralysis (an inability to walk, for example). The virus is shed in a person's feces and is often transmitted through ingesting contaminated water.

Paradoxically, improved sanitation led to an *increase* in the number of children who contracted the disease. In the days before modern sewage treatment, most people were exposed to the polio virus early in their lives and developed immunity (resistance) to the disease. But with improved sanitation, young children were no longer exposed during infancy and so did not develop immunity. As a result, they got a much more serious case of the disease later in childhood—often from swimming in public pools. Polio reached a peak in the United States during the 1950s. Luckily, a vaccine exists now that prevents children from contracting the disease.

courage comes in the four year size...

FIGHT INFANTILE PARALYSIS

NATIONAL FOUNDATION FOR INFANTILE PARALYSIS, INC.
INC. 120 Broadway, New York 5, N.Y.

Schistosomiasis (SHIS-toh-so-MY-uh-sis): Also known as **bilharzia** (bill-HAR-zee-a), this cheery disease is caused by tiny parasitic worms that invade your body when your skin comes in contact with contaminated freshwater. If an infected person urinates or defecates in the water, the water becomes contaminated with schistosome eggs. The eggs hatch, and if a certain kind of microscopic snail is present in the water, the parasites enter the snails' bodies and grow inside them. The parasites grow into worms that can penetrate a person's skin. Within several weeks, these worms begin to grow inside a person's body, leading to fever, muscle pains, and sometimes death.

Typhoid (tie-foyd): High fever, a spotty rash, killer diarrhea—it's a notoriously deadly affliction. Typhoid germs can be easily transferred by a victim who hasn't washed his or her hands after using the bathroom. You can also get it when flying insects feed on infected feces and then transfer the bacteria onto your food.

Typhoid has killed millions of people over the course of human history. Even today, the disease strikes as many as twenty-two million people a year.

Sometimes people can have typhoid but not feel sick. They may not even know they have it. These "chronic carriers" continue to shed the bacteria in their feces and can cause new outbreaks to occur for years. Typhoid Mary is the most famous example (see page 21). Mary Mallon, a cook in New York, probably gave the disease to several hundred people before doctors figured out that she was the source of infection.

BAD-NEWS BUGS

FLEAS: Can cause plague.

FLIES: Can transmit as many as thirty different diseases, including dysentery, cholera, and typhoid.

MOSQUITOES: Can transmit dengue fever, malaria, and encephalitis.

LICE: Can transmit typhus.

BEDBUGS, TICKS, AND COCKROACHES: Awful, disgusting, and horrible as they are, they can't be blamed for pandemics (widespread diseases). But ticks can transmit Lyme disease, and cockroach excrement and body parts can cause severe reactions in people with asthma.

DON'T LET THE BEDBUGS BITE

THERE ARE INSECTS THAT cause direct injury, such as bedbugs, mosquitoes, horseflies, and bees. These insects can cause maddening itching, painful stings, or just a disconcerting feeling of being eaten for dinner.

But insects can also cause *indirect* injury, and these are the real threats to human health. These types of insects are known as vectors—they transmit disease-causing organisms. Germs hop aboard the bug, which then bites and infects a human. For example, fleas are vectors of plague, houseflies are vectors of typhoid, mosquitoes are vectors of malaria. We know this now, but earlier in history people had no idea that the vermin buzzing around their cesspits and midden heaps (see page 14) were responsible for transmitting these diseases.

NOTABLE VICTIMS OF "FILTH" DISEASES

Cholera: Tchaikovsky (see page 119), President James K. Polk, and Alexandre Dumas.

Malaria: Genghis Khan, Dante, and Oliver Cromwell. Many U.S. presidents suffered periodic bouts of malaria throughout their lifetime, including George Washington, James Monroe, Abraham Lincoln, Ulysses S. Grant, and Theodore Roosevelt.

Polio: President Franklin D. Roosevelt.

Typhoid: Pericles, Alexander the Great, and Franz Schubert probably all succumbed to typhoid, as did Prince Albert (Queen Victoria's husband), Wilbur Wright (of the Wright brothers), and two of Louis Pasteur's daughters.

Typhus: Anne Frank and countless soldiers, prisoners, and concentration camp victims.

LICE, LICE POOP, AND TYPHUS

LICE HAVE BEEN BUGGING humans since caveman days. In Egyptian tombs, mummified lice and nits (the eggs of lice) have been found on mummified human hosts. Hair combs dating back to 100 BC, dug up by archaeologists in Israel, show evidence of lice.

Of two types of lice that afflict humans—head lice and body lice—the body louse is the better disease vector. It prefers to live in clothing and can exist away from its human host for a long time.

Although the bites are unpleasant and cause intense itching, it's the *other* end of the insect that really causes trouble. The feces of the louse contain infectious parasites. The feces dry quickly when exposed to air and turn into a fine, parasite-laden dust that can easily enter a human's body through the skin, lungs, or mouth and infect it with typhus. Typhus strikes most often when people live in unsanitary, crowded conditions such as concentration camps or soldiers' barracks.

When Napoleon Bonaparte set out in June of 1812 to conquer Russia, he marched with 500,000 troops. By the end of the failed campaign later that year, as many as 220,000 of those men had died of typhus.

Typhus also killed three million people in Russia and Poland between 1918 and 1922.

A really
BAD
hair day.

"TYPHOID MARY"

Mary Mallon—known as "Typhoid Mary"—was a cook in New York who probably gave the disease to several hundred people before doctors figured out that she was the source of infection.

FLEAS AND DISEASE

GARBAGE AND EXCREMENT ATTRACT rats. Rats attract fleas. Some types of fleas can cause terrible diseases—most notably, plague.

You catch bubonic (boo-BON-ik) plague by getting bitten by a diseased flea. An oozy, pus-filled blister appears at the site of the flea bite, and the nearest lymph nodes start to swell, harden, and turn black, eventually forming lemon-size buboes (lumps). Before the discovery of antibiotics, bubonic plague killed two-thirds of the people who became infected with it.

HYGIENE HEROES

Neatnik Nurse
FLORENCE NIGHTINGALE

During the Crimean War (1853–1856) there were far more deaths caused by typhus than by battle wounds. Florence Nightingale was a British nurse who saved untold numbers of lives by introducing basic sanitation as a standard hospital practice. Although she had no idea that lice were the source of typhus, her insistence on cleanliness greatly reduced louse populations and, therefore, reduced the spread of the disease.

· 3 ·
The Origin of Feces

ANCIENT HISTORY

HUMANS HAVE BEEN AROUND for about two million years, but it was not until relatively recently—about six thousand years ago—that they started writing things down. Everything that happened before that is known as prehistoric times. How can we learn about ancient people who left no written record of their daily lives? One way is to study ancient poop.

ICKY OCCUPATIONS

1

PALEOSCATOLOGISTS

Paleoscatologists are scientists who spend a lot of time on the job studying ancient poop. Their word for a specimen of ancient excrement is "coprolite." Believe it or not, they learn a lot from the fossilized human excrement at the end of their pooper-scooper—such as what people ate and what diseases they carried.

DINOPOOP

A SIXTY-FIVE-MILLION-YEAR-OLD coprolite deposited by a T. rex contained traces of another dinosaur, which the T. rex had eaten for dinner. The fossilized dinosaur turd was the size of a loaf of bread.

PREHISTORIC PORTA POTTIES

EARLY HUMANS PROBABLY DIDN'T worry too much about where they relieved themselves. For a few hundred thousand years, our prehistoric ancestors kept pretty busy moving from place to place, chasing herds of animals. Their troubles began as soon as they stopped roaming and settled down in one place.

THE DAWN OF CIVILIZATION

ABOUT TWELVE THOUSAND YEARS ago, humans abandoned their hunter-gatherer way of life and began to settle down in villages. Around four thousand years ago, villages began to band together and grow bigger, forming ever-larger towns, which grew into cities. The first cities arose in the area between the Tigris and Euphrates rivers, in what is now the country of Iraq. For the first time in human history, people could no longer move away from their waste, as they had always done. In permanent settlements, it was the waste rather than the people that had to move. As cities grew bigger, so did the sanitation problems.

Professional water carriers had to lug their heavy loads through uneven streets, up and down stairs, and in terrible weather.

PIOUS POTTY TRAINING

NOWADAYS MOST PEOPLE OVER the age of ten consider it impolite to talk about pooping. The process of eliminating waste is something generally done behind closed doors. But not so long ago, pooping was a more public activity. Hardly anyone had rooms dedicated exclusively to relieving themselves. In ancient Rome, people sat side by side in open rooms, chatting and pooping. (See "Pooping in Public," page 36, for more on Roman toilet practices.) And for centuries, even in fine homes, chamber pots and closestools could be found right in the dining room.

And consider the Bible. Potty talk is all over the Old Testament. Proper poop disposal was a big issue, even thirty-six hundred years ago. In Deuteronomy, God, through Moses, instructs the Hebrews to carry a shovel when they go off to relieve themselves:

And thou shalt have a paddle among thy weapons; and it shall be, when thou sittest down abroad, thou shalt dig therewith, and shalt turn back and cover that which cometh from thee.

A GREAT place for ancient Romans to catch up on the latest gossip!

HOLY BUT UNHEALTHY

In 1947, Bedouin tribesmen discovered ancient scrolls in a cave near the Dead Sea, about ten miles from Jerusalem. These Dead Sea Scrolls, as they came to be called, were created between 250 BC and 68 AD. They are believed to have been created by a small group of monks called the Essenes. Archaeologists also found latrines used by the monks nearby and concluded that the monks' toileting practices exposed them to large numbers of intestinal parasites. Unlike the local Bedouins, who defecated aboveground, the Essenes dug holes and buried their waste outside the city. (They were also not allowed to defecate on the Sabbath.)

When scientists took samples at the latrine site, they found evidence of ancient roundworms, tapeworms, whipworms, and pinworms—unwelcome, nutrient-devouring worms that can set up shop inside a person's intestinal canal. Because the waste had been buried, the parasites had thrived. (Had the monks defecated aboveground like everyone else, their waste would have dried quickly in the sun, killing the parasites.) As a result, the Essenes were a very sickly bunch. Fewer than 6 percent of them lived to be older than forty.

Dead Sea Scrolls, but no toilet paper rolls.

THOSE HAPPENING HARRAPANS

MANY HISTORIANS CONSIDER THE official start of human civilization to be the time when people started to write stuff down. But you could also argue that civilization began with the first toilet.

The Harrapans were probably the earliest civilization to figure it out—they built the first pipes and sewer systems roughly five thousand years ago.

The Harrapan civilization lived in the valley of the Indus River, in what is now the country of Pakistan, and they dominated the region for two thousand years. During that time they built some impressive cities. The cities of Harrapa and Mohenjo-Daro, built about 2500 BC, had complex drainage systems beneath the streets. While Europeans were still living in caves, this civilization built private houses as well as public bathhouses with pipes that drained into covered sewers. (As a point of reference, the concept of putting covers over smelly sewers wouldn't occur to Parisians for about four thousand more years.)

A FEAT IN CRETE

THE MINOANS LIVED ON Crete—an island near Greece—about four thousand years ago, and they knew how to live in style. They built elegant homes, lavish palaces—and sophisticated plumbing systems. Minoan plumbers figured out how to make water flow out of a tap. Then they went a step further and invented a flushing toilet, which relied on gravity—rainwater was collected in cisterns and flowed down from the roof. In the ruins of their ancient palaces, these toilets still exist and can *still flush*. But this luxury was just for the king.

EGYPT: PYRAMIDS BUT NO POTTIES

THE ANCIENT EGYPTIANS BUILT an empire that spanned three thousand years. They were no slouches when it came to building glorious monuments to the afterlife, such as gigantic pyramids. But they weren't particularly interested in plumbing.

So, what did Egyptians do when they had to relieve themselves? Rich people sat on a limestone seat with a hole in it. The waste fell into a sand-filled vase, and the

contents were disposed of by servants. Regular Egyptians just dumped their waste into the Nile or squatted outside. Desert scavengers—such as rodents, birds, and insects—took care of whatever waste was left lying around.

DUNG BEETLE BEHAVIOR

ONE SORT OF SCAVENGER you are likely to find in the Sahara Desert is the dung beetle. *Coleoptera scarabaeidae*, or the scarab, as it is more commonly known, will locate a pile of dung and create a ball out of it. Then it will roll the dung ball into its nest, where the female lays an egg on it. When the egg hatches, the larva that emerges will burrow into and eat the dung ball.

• Scarabs were worshipped by the ancient Egyptians. Egyptians saw scarabs as a symbol of rebirth.

• Today, dung beetles are found all over the world, and we have a lot to thank them for. People who live in warmer climates would be up to their chins in waste without these efficient little recyclers.

• One scientist (who evidently had some time on his hands) counted *16,000 dung beetles* in a single heap of elephant poop.

• How do dung beetles reproduce? They usually meet in the dung pat. The male offers the female a giant-size ball of poop. If she accepts his gift, they roll the ball away together or the female rides on the ball.

TOO MUCH INFORMATION? TMI

CLEAN UP THAT MESS-OPOTAMIA!

AROUND THE SAME TIME as the Egyptians (3000 BC–550 BC), another civilization, known as Mesopotamia, was busy evolving in the area that is now Iraq. Its teeming, sophisticated cities were bustling trade centers that dominated much of the ancient world. Over time, Mesopotamia was conquered by tribe after tribe and ruled by a succession of kings and tribes, including the Sumerians, Babylonians, Assyrians, and Hittites. What's one big reason for Mesopotamia's success? Good plumbing. Since Mesopotamians tended to be a bit more pessimistic than the Egyptians about the prospect of a glorious afterlife, they were better about cleaning things up in the here and now. Many of its rulers made sanitation a priority.

The Babylonian king Nebuchadnezzar (neh-buh-kuhd-NEH-zur), who lived about 630–562 BC, was one of the more visionary rulers of his day. He had canals dug and cisterns built. Wealthier Babylonians actually had toilets installed in their homes. The toilets were placed over terra-cotta drainage pipes and probably worked reasonably well. Most poor Mesopotamians relieved themselves by squatting outside. Disease was probably not a big problem as the waste would have dried quickly in the hot sun, killing most of the harmful elements.

King Nebuchadnezzar was an ancient clean freak.

HAIR TODAY, GONE TOMORROW

THE HITTITES REALIZED THAT WATER MIGHT carry germs and other impurities, so they made sure that their kings always drank strained drinking water. When one Hittite king found a hair in his water jug, he had the water carrier put to death.

· 4 ·

An Ionic Twist: Poor Plumbing in Ancient Greece

GREEKY CLEAN

ATHENS WAS THE HAPPENING city-state back in ancient Greece. Its society was way ahead of those everywhere else by the standards of the day. Notable Athenian citizens excelled at poetry, art, architecture, philosophy, playwriting, math, medicine, and

forming democratic governments. But they were not especially good at managing the waste that piled up around the city.

It also must be said that most people living in Athens were excluded from participating in the democracy. Only free males could be citizens, and they made up just 15 percent of the population—which left the other 85 percent of the people living in Athens out of the loop: namely, women, slaves, commoners, and foreigners. And in spite of the impressive aqueducts that channeled water into bathhouses and public fountains, most Athenian homes had no running water. So, while the rich male aristocrats were lounging around the bathhouse contemplating philosophy, the foreigners, women, commoners, and slaves were busy staggering back from the local fountain, carrying heavy urns full of water or emptying chamber pots in the streets.

The two major city-states, Athens and Sparta, were plagued by overcrowding and bad sanitation. As a result, the populations of both cities frequently suffered from terrible epidemics. When especially deadly diseases swept the city, Athenians blamed the Spartans, accusing them of poisoning the water. But the diseases were more likely caused by dirty water, insects, and general filth.

HELLENIC HYGIENE

SOAP WAS NOT USED IN GREEK BATHHOUSES. Slaves rubbed people down with oil and ashes or scrubbed them with pumice and sand. A curved bronze tool called a *strigil* was used to scrape the body clean.

Greek baths used a system that provided both hot and cold water, but most Greek warriors took only cold showers—hot was for Macedonian wimps.

Wearing a robe (called a *chiton*) posed challenges for you if you were riding in your chariot (it tended to get caught in the wheels), but it made it easy to squat over a chamber pot. Greeks were not bothered by underwear bunching at their ankles—they didn't wear any.

Bare-bottomed babies could be held out of windows if mothers (or slaves) were quick enough to realize the baby needed to go. But ancient Greek caregivers might also have employed something like this unique stone kiddy potty.

WINE

THE GREEKS WERE AWARE that drinking contaminated water was dangerous to their health. Whenever possible, they drank rainwater collected in water tanks. They also drank a lot of wine. They may or may not have known that wine has natural antibacterial properties, but they knew that wounds were less likely to become infected if they were cleaned with wine rather than with water.

ICKY OCCUPATIONS

2

GREEK SLAVE

Most **Greek slaves** were born free but became slaves for one reason or another. Some had parents who were too poor to take care of them and had sold them. Others had been kidnapped as children. Still others were prisoners of war. Although some slaves enjoyed a fairly decent life, all slaves had to do what their masters told them to. Some worked at the baths, scrubbing down naked people's bodies with sand or pumice stones. Some carried water. Others were rowers in the stinking dark galleys of ships. The worst job for slaves was working in the silver mines—these slaves usually came from fierce northern barbarian tribes. It was dangerous, exhausting work, and most died within a few years from overwork and lead poisoning.

· 5 ·
When in Rome, Poo as the Romans Do

THE ETRUSCANS

ABOUT 700 BC, THE area that would become Rome was little more than marshland. A few tribal sheepherders (Latins and Sabines) had settled in small clusters of houses around the boggy banks of the Tiber River. But then a civilization of people called the Etruscans moved in. They were so good at draining land that the settlement grew rapidly into a city. The Etruscans built Rome's first sewers somewhere between 625 BC and 575 BC. These sewers drained the swampy areas around the river and enabled the lower-lying parts of the city to dry out and be built on.

ICKY OCCUPATIONS

3 ETRUSCAN SEWER DIGGER

Digging sewers out of swampland was hot, buggy, backbreaking work. Etruscan kings probably used slaves for this unpleasant job, as well as semiforced labor from the poorer citizens of Rome. There was so much work to be done that most laborers spent the bulk of their wretched lives digging. Quite a few workers chose to commit suicide rather than face such a dismal future. As a result, one king decreed that anyone who committed suicide would have his body crucified, remaining unburied and picked over by vultures. The prospect of such a disgraceful end was enough to curb the trend.

SHORT ATTENTION SPAN? SOME RAPID ROMAN HISTORY

AFTER THE ETRUSCANS CAME THE ROMAN REPUBLIC; then there was a slight setback when Rome was sacked by the Gauls in 387 BC. The city was rebuilt in a hurry, eventually giving rise to the mighty Roman Empire.

TOILETS AND THE RISE OF THE EMPIRE

WHAT MADE THE ROMAN Empire great? You have to give at least some credit to good plumbing. The Romans built sewers and laid pipes in every territory they conquered. Unlike in other large cities of the ancient world, where waste piled up with nowhere to go, Roman sewers washed a lot of the waste into the Tiber River and eventually out to sea. Roman plumbers also built public toilets—by 315 AD there were more than a million people living in Rome, with 144 public toilets throughout the city.

Roman engineers proved to be masterful plumbers. As the empire grew and expanded, the Romans built magnificent aqueducts and superb sewer systems. Huge underground vaulted tunnels helped drain away rainwater and refuse. What's more, many of their aqueducts and sewers are still in use today. Roman plumbing became the gold standard that future generations could only try to imitate.

Built to last.

WE'RE NOT MAKING THIS UP

THE ROMANS HAD A GODDESS OF SEWERS, whose name was Venus Cloacina. They also had a god of dung. His name was Stercutius. Presumably fertilizer-worshipping farmers prayed to him.

THE GLORY DAYS OF THE EMPIRE

THE ROMAN EMPIRE LASTED more than five hundred years. At its height, the empire extended from Africa all the way to England (which Rome conquered in 43 AD). And everywhere they went, the Roman plumbers got busy.

In Britain, they laid pipes and built aqueducts. In the town of Bath, where there were huge natural hot springs, they built magnificent marble bathhouses.

Romans were the first to use lead pipes to transport water. Before that, pipes had been made of terra-cotta or wood. As the empire grew more and more lavish, bathhouses grew immense—sometimes covering twenty square acres—and had hot, cold, and warm running water. The hot water was heated by furnaces beneath the brick floor.

The Latin word *plumbus* means "lead," which is where we get our word for plumbing.

POOPING IN PUBLIC

ROMANS WERE NOT SHY about bodily functions, to say the least. Very often, going to the toilet was a public activity, a place to hang out with friends and gossip. Ruins of Roman privies show that there were as many as twenty marble seats. The seats were set side by side, with no dividers. Some of the fancier latrines even had heated seats. Often the latrines were built over running streams or over artificially running water that had been channeled to run below the toilet seats.

For travelers who needed to relieve themselves, urns, called *gastra*, were placed along the side of the road—ancient Roman rest stops.

ICKY OCCUPATIONS

4

FULLER

Fullers were the ancient equivalent of modern-day dry cleaners—they removed oil and dirt from cloth, softened it up, and cleaned it. To soften and clean the cloth, fullers used human urine. Urine is 98 percent water, but it also contains ammonia, which is an excellent cleaning and softening agent. Fullers placed large urns on many street corners throughout the city, and men were invited to urinate into them. The urine was then collected and put on a shelf for a couple of weeks. The result was stinking, stale urine, extra strong from evaporation. To clean cloth, the fuller dumped the urine into a vat, threw in the cloth, hoisted up his toga, and stepped into the vile-smelling liquid. He then stomped around on the cloth for an hour or two. Presto! Clean, soft toga cloth!

THE SHORT END OF THE STICK

ANCIENT ROMANS DID NOT use toilet paper. Instead, public bathrooms had a bucket of salt water, into which a sponge on a stick had been placed. You used the sponge to wipe yourself, then returned it to the bucket for the next guy.

RICHER ROMANS

YOU'VE PROBABLY HEARD ABOUT the famously decadent Roman banquets. It was acceptable—actually, expected—for banqueters to follow the "dictates of nature." This is just a fancy way of saying they were permitted to fart, burp, and spit as much as they liked.

Diners who needed to relieve themselves during a banquet simply called over a slave. The slave would help them use a silver urn as a chamber pot (or as a vomit receptacle, depending on the diner's preference), which they would use in full view of the other banqueters.

In private homes, toilets were often a hole in the floor connected to a vertical sewer pipe. It was easy enough to hoist one's robes up to squat over the hole.

POOR ROMANS

ALTHOUGH IT'S TRUE THAT many wealthier Roman citizens bathed in running water and relieved themselves in ornately designed public toilets, don't assume all Romans enjoyed such luxuries. Poor people lived in cramped apartment buildings called *insulae,* which were slum dwellings that had no heat or water. The *insulae* were haphazardly built structures, so closely packed that the areas between them were hardly streets at all. The streets were twisty, narrow, dark, and vile smelling. Some *insulae* could be as high as six stories, and all water had to be carried up by hand from the ground floor. One *insula* was ten stories tall—the first skyscraper of sorts. Because of their shoddy construction, *insulae* frequently collapsed or caught fire. And with no available source of water, fires were disastrous.

The ground floor of some *insulae* contained public latrines known as *foricae.* But many dwellings had no toilets at all.

ICKY OCCUPATIONS

5

TANNER

Tanning is a process in which animal skins (hides) are chemically altered so that they can be made into leather. Back in the days of ancient Rome, this was a complicated and time-consuming procedure. First, the tanners soaked the hide in water. Then they pounded and scoured the skin to remove the rotten flesh and fat. (Imagine the smell.) Next came a long soak in concentrated urine, which loosened up the hair fibers so that the fur could be scraped off. (Imagine the smell.) After that, the tanners mixed up a big vat of dog doo and pigeon dung and smeared the hide with the mixture. They then gave it another good soaking, smooshing, and pounding. (Maybe we should stop imagining the smell.)

Why did early tanners soak hides in poop? There was (and still is) something in the composition of excrement that helped to soften and strengthen the leather. The softening agents come from bacteria found in the digestive tracts of animals.

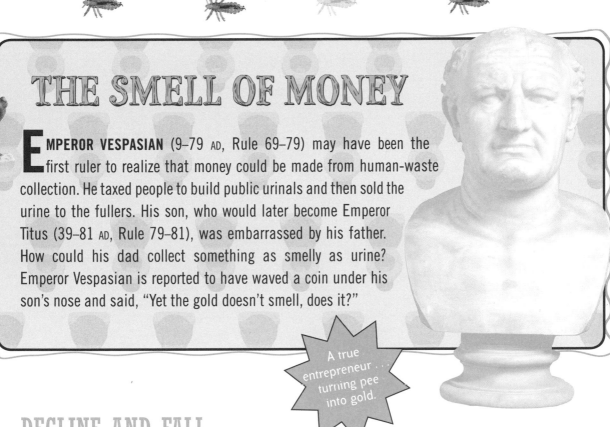

THE SMELL OF MONEY

EMPEROR VESPASIAN (9–79 AD, Rule 69–79) may have been the first ruler to realize that money could be made from human-waste collection. He taxed people to build public urinals and then sold the urine to the fullers. His son, who would later become Emperor Titus (39–81 AD, Rule 79–81), was embarrassed by his father. How could his dad collect something as smelly as urine? Emperor Vespasian is reported to have waved a coin under his son's nose and said, "Yet the gold doesn't smell, does it?"

A true entrepreneur . . . turning pee into gold.

DECLINE AND FALL

IN TIME, THE ROMAN EMPIRE collapsed. Some historians have conjectured that Rome's decline was caused by its citizens' reliance on lead pipes. Lead is known to be a poisonous substance. It's even been suggested that the demented behavior of some of the emperors might have been caused by lead poisoning.

POISONED OR NOT?

SINCE LEAD POISONING TENDS to build up in bones, scientists studied the bones of ancient Romans to see how much lead is concentrated in them. Some studies did reveal that the bones had elevated lead levels. But the buildup of lead is unlikely to have come from the drinking water. Ancient Roman pipes were probably lined with calcium deposits, which would have prevented lead from entering the drinking water, at least somewhat. On the other hand, there was plenty of lead in the pottery and other food-storage containers that the Romans used. So perhaps it's possible that the deranged behavior of some of the emperors *may* have been caused by lead-induced dementia.

If we allow that lead poisoning *may* have factored into the behavior of Rome's rulers, can we blame lead poisoning for the fall of Rome? Maybe in part. But Rome's decline was also helped along by bad sanitation in overcrowded neighborhoods. Throw in earthquakes, volcanoes, and several thousand Visigoth invaders, and you've got a recipe for disaster. After the appropriately named Vandals finished off Rome in 455 AD and the Saxons sacked Bath in 577 AD, things went from bad to worse. Diseases carried off another huge portion of Rome's population, and that was pretty much that.

The barbarians destroyed most of the Roman hot pools and elaborately laid pipes, so the secrets of good plumbing were lost to the Western world. Another thirteen hundred years would pass before real toilet innovations would reappear.

· 6 ·

The Age of Shovelry: Poop in the Middle Ages

"Did I have to drink that second flagon of mead?"

KNIGHTS IN GRIMY ARMOR

AH, KNIGHTS, FAIR DAMSELS, courtly love. Castles, moats, the Age of Chivalry. There are some who would say the Middle Ages were a great time to be alive. Well, they would be wrong. People who lived in the Middle Ages—spanning the time from roughly 500 to 1500 AD—could look forward to a short life expectancy, wars, famines, plagues, persecution, religious fanaticism, and an entire lifetime spent in slavelike servitude, at least for 90 percent of the population. Oh, and also lots of insect bites.

What's more, human waste was a constant presence in people's lives, no matter how wealthy they were. If they were poor, the waste was heaped up both inside and outside their homes. If they were rich, it was probably piled just outside or dumped in the moat, if they lived in a castle.

You've probably seen movies set in days of yore, in which attractive lords and ladies clop on horseback along clean cobblestone streets. Don't let those movies fool you. Actual medieval towns looked nothing like this. They were crowded with unwashed, pockmarked people, trudging along narrow, muddy streets, past dead and decaying animals, stagnant pools of water, and piles of human excrement. And those were the nicer towns.

EARLY MIDDLE AGES

AFTER THE FALL OF ROME, barbarian tribes slashed their way across Europe and the British Isles. For several hundred years, on and off, they hacked away, killing one another as well as any unfortunate peasants who happened to get in their way. Meanwhile, because barbarian tribes had embraced Christianity pretty early on, the power of the Catholic Church grew stronger. The leaders of the church disapproved of ancient Greek and Roman societies, with their worship of pagan gods. So anything Greek or Roman fell out of favor. Since the barbarians had destroyed most of the Roman sewers and aqueducts, Roman plumbing technology sank into obscurity.

Farther to the East, Byzantine rulers had the sense to preserve Roman technology, and as a result, their people enjoyed a higher sanitary standard of living (more on these cities later).

WHAT NOT TO WEAR IN MEDIEVAL EUROPE: ROMAN TOGAS

BECAUSE THINGS ROMAN WERE OUT OF STYLE, togas became a major fashion don't. Simpler "Christian dress" was a much safer option if you didn't care to be persecuted as a heretic. In northern climates, men started wearing trousers or leggings. These fashions made the Roman-style habit of squatting over a hole in the floor difficult. So chamber pots became the toilet of choice for the nobility. Early chamber pots were made of earthenware or tin.

HYGIENE BECOMES UNHOLY

THE UPSIDE OF BEING a Christian during the Middle Ages was that you were no longer in danger of being thrown to the lions, as you might have been if you had lived during the Roman Empire. The downside was that being a Christian meant you were more or less expected to stop washing yourself. Christians believed that washing one's body was sinful. Warm water might cause impure thoughts, so it was best avoided. Back then, uncleanliness was next to godliness—in that bad hygiene sent a lot of people to their Maker sooner rather than later.

St. Benedict (480-543 AD) drew up a list of rules for Christians. One declared that "bathing shall seldom be permitted."

WHILE YOU WERE HEAPING

AS WITH MOST MEDIEVAL CITIES, a huge wall surrounded Paris. Human waste was collected in carts and dumped outside the wall. But as the population grew, so did the dung piles. Periodically the walls had to be built higher so that attackers would not be able to run up the sides of the dung heaps and over the walls.

TOO MUCH INFORMATION?
TMI

THE DECLINE OF EMPIRES AND THE RISE OF FEUDALISM

BY 800 OR SO, Charlemagne had become the leader of the Frankish Empire (the area that is now France), and his power extended across much of Western Europe. But after his death, a series of weak successors managed to send the Frankish Empire into decline. Judging from some of their names (Charles the Bald, Louis the Stammerer, Charles the Fat, Charles the Simple), this should have been a surprise to no one.

With the collapse of the Frankish Empire, the Western world changed. No longer was it dominated by huge empires like those of the ancient Persians, Greeks, and Romans. Now instead of major urban centers, smaller territories sprang up around Europe and Britain. Anyone with land and money hastily built a castle to protect themselves and their property from marauding invaders. It was sensible to build your castle high up on a hilltop in order to be able to spot enemies approaching. Meanwhile, Viking warriors on warships zoomed inland along every river, wreaking havoc on European towns.

An uphill battle? Walls could keep residents safe from invaders, but they could also be used by enemies to trap people until they ran out of food or water.

With no central government to protect them, battle-weary peasants turned to their local noblemen for protection. Villages sprang up close to the castles, and residents built walls around their towns for protection. Most people's main focus was trying not to die. Good hygiene became a secondary concern. Living on hilltops and building high walls did help make people feel more secure about not being killed by Vikings, but these medieval architectural trends posed some major challenges. For one thing, how do you get water to flow uphill? For another, where do you put all the poop?

ICKY OCCUPATIONS 6

GONGFERMOR

One of the better-paying medieval jobs was to rake up poop and cart it away. In private houses, servants dumped chamber pots into pits in the backyard, which were called privy pits. These pits needed to be emptied periodically, which was a disgusting task, but **gongfermors** (later known as night-soil men) were happy to have the work. Gongfermors climbed right down into the muck and shoveled the stuff into barrels, which they then carted out of town. The job was usually done in the middle of the night. Since it was a big expense for most households, people tended to wait until their privy pit was full or overflowing before they hired someone to empty it. So a gongfermor's horse usually had a heavy load to pull. Sometimes, to save the horse's strength, the driver lightened the load by drilling a hole in the bottom of the barrel so that a trail of poop dribbled out as he headed out of town. This made the gongfermor unpopular with the townspeople.

If there was a farm close by, gongfermors might sell their night soil to the farmer for use as fertilizer. If not, they just carted the waste outside the walls of town and dumped it into a big pile. Visitors approaching some towns could smell these piles from miles away.

EVERY MANOR FOR ITSELF

SO, AS THE MIDDLE AGES progressed, practically every European hilltop had its own fiefdom (mini-kingdom), a castle built by some tough-guy overlord, defended by a knight or two, and largely propped up, economically, by hardworking, overtaxed peasants. This political system of government is known as feudalism, and it lasted for centuries. Peasants built their meager huts near the castle walls, farmed the lands owned by the nobleman, then paid their nobleman protection money in the form of taxes, which amounted to most or all of what they earned from farming. In exchange, the nobleman pledged (with varying degrees of sincerity) to help them not die if the town got attacked.

LIFE IN MEDIEVAL TOWNS

THE WALLS THAT SURROUNDED medieval towns were useful for protecting the inhabitants from attackers. If you travel to Europe, you can visit these towns, many of which still exist and are charming and lovely, with quaint shops and terrific restaurants. But they didn't always look so clean. During the Middle Ages, life inside those walled-in towns could be extremely cramped and unpleasant. Populations grew, but the amount of available space inside the walls remained the same.

To maximize space, buildings were put up close together, creating narrow streets. Some were hardly wider than a man's shoulders. Many buildings were built so that the second floor jutted out over the first, and the third over the second, until it was possible for a flea to jump from a person on an upper floor on one side of the street to a person standing on an upper floor across the street, with little effort by the flea.

A good place to hang out?

Sunlight rarely made it to street level, and at night there was no light at all. Toilets were nonexistent.

SMELLS

BECAUSE THE STREETS SMELLED SO AWFUL, many people walked around holding clove-spiked oranges or aromatic mixtures of herbs and spices enclosed in little balls called pomanders under their noses. Perfume and incense were used liberally to cover the smell of unwashed bodies. Soap was made of animal fat, urine, lye, and ashes—and it smelled revolting. It was rarely used to clean the body. People did use soap to wash clothes occasionally, although they more commonly used urine. Urine contains ammonia, which is a handy cleaning agent. (See "Fuller" box, page 36.)

PRIVIES FOR THE PRIVILEGED

BETTER HOMES SOMETIMES HAD privies (rooms with nonflushing toilets) built off the master bedroom. Usually the waste dropped through a chute into a barrel or trench next to the house. Those who could afford an extra set of clothes often hung their nicer woolen wear in the privy, believing that the smells would drive away moths. Probably as a result of this practice, a medieval privy became known as a "garderobe" (GAR-drōb), which means "a room where clothes are kept."

CASTLE GARDEROBES

IF YOU LIVED IN a castle, your garderobe would be a small room that jutted out from the castle wall. Inside the room was a seat with a hole cut out of it. The seat was made of wood or stone. The seat hole was sometimes suspended over nothingness or, in castles built later, might have been connected to a chute. Either way, that seat must have been awfully cold to sit on in the winter. The waste dropped down in free fall or through the chute into the moat. If there was no moat, it tumbled down the outer castle wall onto the ground or into a barrel or a pit.

People did wash up after relieving themselves. But as most castles were built on hilltops, washing one's hands under running water was out of the question. Donkey wheels were used to draw water up from wells by the bucketful, which was then carted into the castle by servants and poured into basins.

Wash your hands—forks haven't been invented yet.

THEY CALL *THAT* A CITY?

COMPARED TO ANCIENT ATHENS OR ROME, the populations of most medieval cities in Europe might strike you as surprisingly low. By the year 1200, London's population was somewhere between sixty and one hundred thousand. The cities of Venice, Florence, and Milan probably also had about one hundred thousand. But most cities had fewer than five thousand inhabitants.

A few cities had considerably larger populations. Constantinople had over a million people. Cairo had over half a million. The Arab capital of Cordoba, in what is now southern Spain, had more than half a million people as well. How were they able to grow so much bigger than other cities of the time? All these cities shared something in common: better plumbing.

Cordoba had three hundred public baths and extensive drainage and sewage systems. Constantinople had great drainage and sanitation. In both cities, the rulers had preserved the old Roman pipes, baths, and aqueducts.

MOATS

MAYBE YOU'VE SEEN CARTOONS showing moats infested with snapping alligators or man-eating fish. In real life moats were stinking, putrid cesspools where no living thing could possibly survive. When the moats got too choked up with sewage or castle inhabitants couldn't deal with the smell anymore, gongfermors were hired to rake them out. When castles were under siege, a few brave marauders tried to swim the moats to gain entrance to the castle.

If your castle happened not to have a moat, no big deal. Your servants just dumped the waste out the window.

MANY KNIGHTS FOUGHT IN THE CRUSADES. The Crusades were a series of Holy Wars fought between Christians and Muslims. Although they were very bloody, and ultimately pointless, one slight upside to the Crusades was that people from the West saw firsthand how much more advanced many of the cities of the East were. Constantinople, Damascus, and Baghdad had much more sophisticated art, architecture, and plumbing than the cities in the West.

Crusading soldiers who managed to survive returned with new knowledge—Gothic arches, funky headgear, and Arab-style beards became all the rage in Europe—although the Crusaders appeared not to have taken much of an interest in Eastern hygiene practices. But the resulting expansion in trade and an increased interest in exploration eventually helped usher in the Renaissance.

THE BLACK DEATH: PESTILENCE AND POOP

IN 1348, BUBONIC PLAGUE—known as the Black Death—swept through Europe, the Near East, and North Africa, having already decimated the populations of India, China, and East Asia. Within two years, it would kill one-third of the population of Europe and probably that many in the Near East and North Africa as well. Victims developed large black swellings (buboes) in their necks, groins, or armpits, and often a black rash spread over much of their body (see "Fleas and Disease," page 22). The spit, vomit, and excrement of a plague victim smelled so horrible that sick people became objects of revulsion rather than pity. Doctors who managed not to die of the disease walked around wearing beaky masks in an often vain attempt to ward off infection.

Although no one knew it at the time, the disease was spread by flea bites. Germ-carrying fleas lived on black rats. The rats fed on the garbage and excrement in the streets. When the sick host rat died, the infected flea hopped onto a human instead. When it bit the human, the bacillus (disease-causing bacteria) entered the person's bloodstream. Since most medieval cities were overcrowded and filthy, the rat population thrived, and the plague spread.

SIR SMELLSALOT

KING HENRY IV OF ENGLAND (1366–1413) insisted that his knights bathe at least once in their lives—as part of the ceremony to become a knight.

King Henry IV— not big on baths.

7 ICKY OCCUPATIONS

BARBER SURGEON

For people living in the Middle Ages, **barber surgeons** were more than just people who cut hair. They knew how to set bones, perform simple operations, and pull out teeth, although patients had an unfortunate tendency to die from shock or infection.

One man might pop in for a shave and to have his teeth cleaned (by scraping them). Another might need a rotten tooth "drawn" out of his mouth. Another, feeling a bit under the weather, might request to have some blood drawn, which meant slicing open one of the man's veins with a not-very-clean knife. The barber surgeon caught the blood in a special basin and then bound up the wound.

Barber surgeons were also called upon to perform operations to remove kidney stones or even to amputate arms and legs from time to time. (Sensible customers knew enough to drink a great deal of brandy before arriving, since anesthesia hadn't been invented yet.) The patient had a fighting chance at survival if the barber surgeon managed to remove the stone or the limb quickly, and if his instruments were reasonably clean.

To advertise their blood-letting skills, barber surgeons often placed buckets of blood extracted from their customers in their shop windows. When the blood in the buckets got too sticky and dark and congealed, the barber surgeon simply pitched it into the street.

Eventually, barber surgeons would advertise their shops with a red and white striped pole, which represents the blood and bandages from surgery.

DISEASE IN SUPERSTITIOUS TIMES

IN THE MIDDLE AGES, the link between filthiness and disease was far from obvious. People still hadn't figured out that living so close to their own waste could cause terrible epidemics. Instead, most people believed that disease was caused by demons or God's wrath or their own sin. It was a time when perfectly rational people believed in ogres, dragons, witches, and trolls. One widely accepted explanation for the Black Death epidemic in fourteenth-century Paris was that it was an astrological problem: Saturn was in the house of Jupiter! Such superstitious beliefs may strike us as absurd, but what were people *supposed* to think when a person could wake up seemingly healthy in the morning and be dead by lunchtime? Because people lacked knowledge of the true sources of disease, chalking up the cause to an evil curse was as good an explanation as any. It would be hundreds of years before people started to understand that their vermin-infested clothing and the piles of filth that contaminated their water supply were major reasons behind the spread of disease. No wonder the most common treatment for most serious diseases was prayer.

MEDIEVAL TOILET PAPER

DIDN'T EXIST.

The rich used wool or hemp.
The poor used grass, stone,
mussel shells, or water.

OUCH!

8

KNIGHT'S SQUIRE

Knight's squires were nobly born knights-in-training, who were sent away from home at about the age of seven. Once he became a teenager, the squire rode alongside his knight into battle. A big part of his job was to get the knight all suited up. This process would take about an hour.

First the squire helped him into a linen shift and under-drawers. Next he unrolled the woolen hose, which were thick, itchy woolen stockings, and attached them to the bottom of the shift. After that, he helped the knight shimmy into a heavy cloth jacket, known as an arming doublet. Finally, he strapped on all the pieces of armor. Presto—dressed to kill!

After the battle, the squire was expected to clean the armor. This could be a nasty job if the knight happened to bleed all over it. Also, since battles sometimes lasted for hours, the knight probably had to relieve himself inside his armor. The squire cleaned off the blood and sweat and poop with a solution of sand, vinegar, and urine.

INQUISITION AND CLEANLINESS

WHEN THE CATHOLIC CHURCH ruled over the Iberian Peninsula (where Spain is), many Jews and Muslims were forced to convert to Christianity. Since both the Jewish and Muslim religions held beliefs that bathing and cleansing were important, members of the Catholic clergy grew suspicious of any converts who looked too clean. They might secretly still be practicing their old religion! During the Spanish Inquisition (which began in 1480 and lasted for several hundred years), clean people sometimes got into big trouble with their Inquisitors, who suspected them of faking their conversion to Christianity and of cleansing themselves for religious reasons. Extremely disagreeable consequences usually followed.

CLOSESTOOLS

The lap of luxury.

TOWARD THE END OF the Middle Ages, rich people stopped using castle garderobes and started using closestools. A closestool was a chair with a chamber pot underneath it—no doubt warmer and more comfortable than the garderobe's stone seat. Closestools were preferred over chamber pots because they enabled people to sit down more comfortably.

Closestools would be the toilet of choice for wealthy people for the next five hundred years. You can still find antique chairs today that once contained a pot. (See "Well, I Declare!" page 87.)

URINE TROUBLE!

THIS WAS A TIME when doctors examined urine they captured in glass urinals to determine what disease a person had. Sometimes they even tasted it.

TOO MUCH INFORMATION?
TMI

DELOUSER

ICKY OCCUPATIONS

9

Vermin such as lice, fleas, ringworm, and bedbugs were a way of life in the Middle Ages. Etiquette books from the time advise people not to pick off bugs in public. "It is unbecoming and not very nice to scratch your head at table, or pick lice and fleas or other vermin from your neck or your back and kill them in front of people." But certain nimble-fingered women made a living as professional **delousers**. Wealthy people lounged around, gossiping in the sun or in front of a fire, while the delousers picked the bugs off them. We owe the words "nitpick" and "lousy" to this loathsome little arthropod.

· 7 ·

The Reeking Renaissance

STILL IN THE DARK AGES, PLUMBINGWISE

THE RENAISSANCE—IT MEANS "rebirth," and it was a remarkable period in history. The Renaissance marked the end of the Middle Ages and was a time when people's interest in art, reasoning, and knowledge was reborn. But they still didn't bathe much, and they still used chamber pots.

Two separate inventors did invent toilets during the Renaissance. But unfortunately no one paid much attention to either of them. Consequently, most people of the Renaissance lived lives similar to those of their medieval predecessors—smelly, brutish, and short.

WASHING UP

IF YOU WERE TO play a word-association game, chances are "good personal hygiene" is not something that would pop into your head when someone says "Renaissance." And there's a reason for that: the average Renaissance-era peasant was just as unwashed as his medieval predecessors were. People still lugged their water into the house from the town pump, and the water was too scarce to be used for anything besides cooking.

People in wealthier homes did not wash their bodies very often, at least by our standards, but they did wash their hands regularly, and, somewhat less regularly, their faces. They used a jug to pour water over their hands into a basin before meals and after defecating.

Clothes washing among the laboring classes was uncommon too. Because so few people owned a second set of clothes, remaining presentable while doing one's laundry could present a thorny problem.

Peasants wore the same itchy, filthy, vermin-infested clothes day after day, so, not surprisingly, skin diseases were common. But even richer people, who could afford multiple outfits, rarely washed their outer finery, which wasn't exactly wash-and-wear. Most wealthy people did wash their linen chemises, which is what they wore underneath their outer garments (no one wore actual underwear).

The job of lugging water usually fell to women and children. To get a sense of how unfun this chore was, try carrying a jug of milk in each hand . . . for about half a mile.

HYGIENE HEROES

Most people during the Renaissance

still believed that diseases were caused by bad air or evil spirits. It's hard to fathom how doctors didn't notice a connection between bad sanitation and disease, particularly when confronted with disease victims who were matted with dirt and crawling with bugs. But one French doctor did put *deux* and *deux* together. Ambroise Paré (1510–1590) firmly believed that washing hands before examining a patient might be a good way to reduce infection. Tragically, few people listened to him.

All Washed Up
AMBROISE PARÉ

EAT, DRINK, AND BE WARY

WATER WAS OFTEN STORED in lead tanks inside people's homes. Not surprisingly, it tasted awful. So people rarely drank water to quench their thirst. This practice turned out to be prudent, since, in addition to tasting bad, most water was also contaminated with sewage. People used water for boiling meats and for making fermented drinks like ale, beer, or wine. (Fermentation is a natural chemical process that involves using yeast to convert sugar into alcohol and carbon dioxide, which accounts for the fizz of many fermented drinks.) Fermented drinks were a much healthier choice because the fermentation process killed many of the germs present in the water.

Water tasted bad all over Europe. In Italy and France, people drank wine. In Germany and England, they drank ale or beer. Ale varied in strength but was usually made from water, malted barley, herbs, and spices.

Everyone drank alcoholic beverages, including small children. Although the strength of these beverages varied—wine was often watered down, and beer was often, but not always, low in alcohol—every man, woman, and child averaged a *gallon* of ale or wine per day, and they sloshed down flagons of the stuff at breakfast, lunch, and dinner.

Still
thirsty?

Remember, too, that people were smaller than they are today. The average peasant man in 1500 stood about five feet tall and weighed about 135 pounds. A modern-day sixth grader could probably see over his head. So this much drink must have resulted in a continuous state of intoxication, ranging from mild to quite impaired.

COFFEE? TEA? CHOCOLATE? NOT YET.

PEOPLE IN CHINA HAVE been drinking tea for about five thousand years. But tea did not arrive in England until the mid-1600s.

Coffee appeared in Constantinople (which today is called Istanbul) in the 1400s, probably from Arabia, and coffeehouses became popular in London and Paris during the 1600s.

Cocoa beans arrived in Spain and Portugal in 1544, as gifts from the Mayan people. But chocolate was a drink reserved for royalty. The Spanish kept their chocolate source a secret for nearly a century. In fact, in 1579 some English pirates searching for gold aboard a Spanish ship mistook the cocoa beans for sheep droppings and burned the highly valuable cargo. The first "chocolate house" opened in London in 1657.

So people didn't have many options when it came to beverages. Milk was full of disease-causing germs in the days before refrigeration and pasteurization (the process of heating milk to a high enough temperature to kill many of the germs). Without water, milk, coffee, tea, or hot chocolate to drink, it makes sense that so many people opted for alcohol.

ROYAL TREATMENTS

QUEEN ELIZABETH, **WHO REIGNED** during the height of the Renaissance, declared that she took a bath once a month, whether she needed to or not. Her cousin and rival, Mary, Queen of Scots, bathed daily in elderberry wine, which she believed improved the look of her skin. But her beauty regimen was suspended when Elizabeth had her executed.

Some English aristocrats washed their faces with their own urine to achieve a smooth complexion.

CLEANLINESS IN CONSTANTINOPLE

IN **MANY CITIES IN** what is now known as the Middle East and the Far East, people were living cleaner, healthier lives, thanks in part to better plumbing. In 1453, the Ottoman Turks besieged the city of Constantinople, the capital of the Byzantine Empire, and captured it. Constantinople became the capital of the Ottoman Empire.

The Ottomans were Muslims, and good hygiene was part of the Islamic culture. The Koran lists many rules that involve washing hands after defecating, before eating, and before prayer.

Constantinople was a thriving city in the 1500s, with considerably cleaner streets and people than its counterparts in European cities. Most people visited the baths on a somewhat regular basis, and the baths had hot and cold water. Life in the city tended to be centered around the palace. The neighborhoods surrounding the palace were arranged according to people's occupations, in districts known as *mahalles*. Some *mahalles*, like those that contained the butchers' and the tanners' shops, could be just as smelly as those in other European cities.

Throughout the city, packs of dogs roamed, eating the rubbish in the streets.

HENRY'S HORRIFIC HYGIENE

IN 1509, HENRY VIII became king of England. You've probably heard at least something about Henry VIII, like the fact that he had six wives. He ate huge amounts of food, and in his later years he weighed over three hundred pounds. He ordered a great many heads to be chopped off, including those of two of his wives. He went to war with France and enraged the pope by getting divorced.

But in spite of his faults, he did make an effort to improve the dismal sanitation situation in his kingdom. During his reign, Parliament passed a number of laws about proper disposal of waste. But since there was nowhere to put it, the laws were seldom enforced.

The king's palace had a huge "house of easement," with twenty-eight toilet seats on two levels. The toilets drained straight into the Thames (the river that runs through the center of London—and it's pronounced "Temz").

Most noblemen seemed not to have bothered with houses of easement. They just continued to use fireplaces, out-of-the-way corners, or balconies as urinals.

HYGIENE HEROES

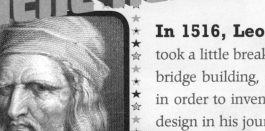

The Da Vinci Commode
LEONARDO DA VINCI

In 1516, Leonardo da Vinci (1452–1519) took a little break from painting, sculpting, designing, bridge building, and solving mathematical theorems in order to invent a toilet that flushed. He drew up a design in his journals for a water closet. His invention even included a ventilation system. Da Vinci intended it to be built in the castle of the French king François I, who was a big fan of da Vinci's work and a major patron of the arts. Unfortunately, da Vinci died in François's palace three years later, leaving behind unrealized toilet sketches and his painting, the *Mona Lisa*, which remains in France to this day. The toilet was never built.

THE ROYAL EASEMENT

HENRY VIII USED A CLOSESTOOL FOR HIS TOILET. He had a servant called the Groom of the Stool, whose job it was to wipe the royal butt.

Queen Elizabeth (Henry's daughter) took her own closestools along with her when she traveled around the countryside. Included in her traveling entourage was a "close carriage"—a portable bathroom.

FASHIONS OF THE TIMES: CODPIECES

PERHAPS ONE OF THE biggest fashion don'ts in history was worn by Renaissance men of the late 1400s to the mid-1500s: the codpiece. The codpiece was a padded crotch covering. It was necessary because the hose men wore left a gap at the top. To cover the gap, a codpiece was buttoned or tied on. It was often elaborately decorated and bizarrely shaped. It could be unfastened to allow the wearer to urinate. Some men had pockets sewn into their codpieces and stored hankies, spare change, and snuff in them.

Eventually "trunk hose" came into fashion, which were balloony pants ending at midthigh that covered up the crotch. But many men still wore codpieces outside their trunk hose. Codpieces finally went out of style by the end of the 1500s, when men started wearing breeches.

ATTENTION, GENTLEMEN

WHEN OUT WALKING WITH A LADY, the gentleman was expected to walk on the side closest to the street, which would mean that he would be the one doused if someone dumped their chamber pot from one of those jutting-out, upper-story windows. He would also be the one more likely to be drenched in filth by a passing carriage.

Meanwhile, most ladies carried parasols, even on cloudy days. It doesn't take much imagination to figure out why this was a good idea.

LOOK OUT BELOW

IT WAS CONSIDERED GOOD MANNERS to warn people on the street below before dumping the contents of one's chamber pot out the window. The cry *Gardez l'eau!* in French means "Watch out for the water!" and may have been mispronounced "gardy-loo." The English word "loo" may or may not have evolved from this expression.

FASHIONS OF THE TIMES: DOES THIS MAKE MY BUTT LOOK BIG?

ORIGINATING IN SPAIN in the mid- to late 1500s, a new fashion appeared for well-to-do women: the farthingale. (It would reappear in a somewhat different shape during the next century.) A farthingale was a stiff contraption, usually a series of hoops made of wood, wire, iron, or whalebone. Its function was to extend the skirt out at right angles from the body—sometimes to a width of four feet. The skirt had to be carefully pinned along the sides and down to the edges of the farthingale, a process that could take hours. In addition to being walking pincushions, wearers became a menace to pedestrians and coffee-table knickknacks; one king tried to have farthingales banned.

It's hard to fathom how a woman could manage to pee while wearing one of these. If she tried to lift up her skirts to sit down on a closestool, she risked jabbing herself in multiple places, only to encounter the stiff barricade of her farthingale. How in the world did a woman manage to pull down underdrawers beneath all that hardware? The answer is she didn't, as women usually didn't wear underwear beneath their skirts and linen undersmocks. Most women just peed standing up.

AT LONG LAST: A ROYAL FLUSH

QUEEN ELIZABETH (1533–1603), Henry VIII's daughter, was on the throne and Shakespeare was busily writing plays when Sir John Harington, who happened to be a godson of the queen, published a pamphlet entitled *The Metamorphosis of Ajax*. It's not clear what "Ajax" refers to; possibly it's a pun on the Elizabethan word for the toilet—"a jakes." In the pamphlet, he drew up a plan for how a flush toilet could be constructed. The queen was offended, and Sir John was banished from court. Eventually, though, he was invited back.

The book was full of dumb puns and potty humor, but nevertheless, his invention was built and installed in the palace. In fact, *two* toilets were built. One was used by the queen herself and the other by Sir John. And they worked! Sort of.

Sir John's toilet was built a hundred years after da Vinci's toilet designs, and the two events comprise the sum total of Renaissance plumbing milestones. A hundred *more* years would go by before anyone tried to improve on Harington's design.

GONE BUT NOT FORGOTTEN

THE EARL OF OXFORD once made a low bow to the Queen and, in doing so, let go a loud fart. He was so ashamed he left the country for *seven years*. When he finally returned, the queen welcomed him back and then said, "My lord, I had forgot the fart."

I AM NOT AMUSED.

BRAAAP!

FASHIONS OF THE TIMES: PATTENS, CHOPINES, GALOSHIOS

MUCKY STREETS LED TO some funky footwear choices. Pattens were platforms made of thick leather or wood, which were strapped to people's shoes to lift them out of the mud and other muck. Chopines were even higher. A galoshio, a sort of backless platform shoe, did the same sort of thing. Sidewalks existed in ancient Rome but had vanished from cities after Rome fell. They would not reappear until the late 1700s. It can't have been easy to walk along wet cobbled streets with pattens strapped to one's feet, or to jump quickly out of the way of a cascading chamber-pot stream.

HYGIENE HEROES

Sir John's John
SIR JOHN HARINGTON

Sir John Harington (1561–1610), the earliest known inventor of a water closet with moving parts, was a popular courtier with a racy sense of humor. He was known as Queen Elizabeth's "saucy godson." (She had 102 godchildren.) But poor Sir John was teased for his efforts and built only two toilets. His invention was way ahead of its time. Without a proper sewage system, a flush toilet was pretty useless anyway, since the flushed waste had nowhere to go.

I'LL TAKE MANHATTAN

TOWARD THE END OF the Renaissance, a rivalry was developing among different countries in Europe. They raced one another to explore and colonize the New World. In particular, the Spanish, Portuguese, English, and Dutch each tried to be the first to lay claim to new territories in North America.

In 1626, a man named Peter Minuit, who was the head of a Dutch trading company, made a deal with the local Indians. At their end of the bargain, the Indians got some cloth, beads, hatchets, and a few other trinkets. In exchange, Minuit got the island of Manhattan. He may or may not have felt he was getting the better deal. After all, Manhattan was an island surrounded by salty water. (Both the Hudson and the East rivers draw in salty water from the ocean tides, mixing ocean salt water with the river freshwater and making the water "brackish," or salty-tasting.) Freshwater had to be drawn from wells and was in relatively short supply. It would be two hundred years before an aqueduct would be built, which piped freshwater into the city from places farther north. Sanitation disposal was already a problem. (It still is.)

> YOU MEAN TO TELL ME I JUST SPENT $28 FOR AN ISLAND WITH NO RUNNING WATER?

Elsewhere in the New World, European settlers made do as best they could in their strange new surroundings. The settlers defecated outdoors, dug cesspits, and built outhouses. They probably missed their chamber pots, which few people had brought with them from the old country—no doubt for space reasons.

NEW WORLD, SAME STUFF

COLONIAL AMERICANS HAD PRETTY slim choices when it came to wholesome beverages. They disliked and distrusted water, just as their European counterparts did. They had no tea, coffee, or chocolate (well into the seventeenth century), and with no refrigeration, milk was not practical. So they drank whiskey, rum, beer, hard cider, and, in the south, peach brandy. In spite of all the laws passed and sermons preached, the colonists were a boozy lot.

· 8 ·

I Smell London, I Smell France

DURING THE SEVENTEENTH CENTURY (the 1600s), London and Paris were two of the most powerful cities in the world. Their problems with sanitation continued to worsen as the century progressed. London suffered from plague and a huge fire, Paris (and the rest of France) from overtaxed peasants and irresponsible rulers, who used the revenue for their own purposes.

Most large cities in Europe and America were experiencing similar problems—filthy streets, high infant mortality, and bad water. It was common for seventeenth-century families to have twelve or thirteen children, but an appalling number of children died before reaching the age of five—and all too often their mothers died too.

THIRSTY?

LET'S SAY IT'S A hot day in London in 1650, and you want a drink of water. By now, wooden water pipes would have been laid underneath London's streets. If your family is well off, you might have paid a fee to be connected to the main pipes. These pipes leak at the joints and make the water that finally trickles through your faucet taste disgusting.

But if you are like most people, your family can't afford to have water piped in. There might be a well in the garden, usually right next to the cesspit. But most likely, you have to lug your water yourself from the nearest street-corner standpipe. Or you can buy your water from a water seller, who might even carry it upstairs for you if you tip him.

PUBLIC POOPING

IN FINER HOMES, THE ladies left the dining room after dinner and retired to closestools, while the men remained behind in the dining room. Servants pulled chamber pots out of cupboards, to be used by the men as they continued chatting. If a guest felt a "greater" urge and the night was fine, he might stroll outside to empty his bowels in the garden somewhere. If the weather was not fine, well, there was always the great indoors—and servants to clean up everything later.

HISTORICAL NAMES FOR POOP— AT LEAST, THE ONES WE'RE ALLOWED TO PRINT

BM
dung
effluvium

excrement
excreta
feces

manure
night soil
ordure

Effluvium

QUITE LOVELY, JEEVES

TRAFFIC

MODERN-DAY LONDON TRAFFIC is famously awful, but during the 1600s it may actually have been worse than it is today, once you factor in all the piles of manure and herds of animals that drivers had to steer around. Remember that back then, the principal vehicles were horses, not cars. There were no sidewalks, no stoplights, no traffic cops, and absolutely no traffic laws. Carriage drivers would see a space open up in the snarl of traffic and dash for it. Main streets didn't get much wider than ten or eleven feet, and often two carts passing in opposite directions were wider than that, so standstills and snarl-ups happened frequently. At night the streets were completely dark.

Huge numbers of people traveled on foot. Most laborers lived close to where they worked, and those who didn't walked back and forth, sometimes over extreme distances. Added to the pedestrians and horse-and-cart traffic were herds of animals driven through the streets on their way to the market—cows, pigs, goats, and chickens, all of which deposited manure—to say nothing of the many *dead* animals that lay where they fell. Most streets had huge signboards hanging nine feet overhead (to allow a rider on horseback to pass beneath). The signs advertised inns, public houses (bars), tooth drawers (primitive dentists), carpenters, and even private homes. There were no house numbers; people would be directed to a location by following the signboards.

PERILS FOR PEDESTRIANS

STROLLING THROUGH THE STREETS of Paris or London was not something you did unless it was absolutely necessary. Smelly industries added to the general noise, traffic, and stench of the city. Tanners, soap makers, glue makers, textile finishers (similar to the Roman fullers of old), and knackers (see "Renderer" box, page 111) all added their own odoriferous smells to the air. But slaughterhouses—called abattoirs—most likely created the worst noises and smells and goriest waste of all. Animal blood and guts were usually tossed into the nearest stream or river or simply onto a big, maggoty pile.

That isn't rain . . . is it?

The smog that hung over the city was created by coal-burning industries and by individual households that used coal for heat and for cooking, creating a murky gloom on even the brightest summer days.

BEWARE OF BATHS

EUROPEANS IN THE SEVENTEENTH and eighteenth centuries were still reluctant to soak in a tub. They thought that the skin was porous, like a sponge. Soaking in a tub opened up the pores and exposed the body to infection.

So baths were taken very infrequently, and usually for medical reasons. If your doctor decided that a bath was necessary, it was a major event in your life and could produce a lot of anxiety. After the bath, doctors usually prescribed a strict regimen for the bather, including days of rest, staying in bed, and wearing protective clothing.

One morning in 1610, Henry IV (the king of France) sent a messenger to one of his ministers, requesting the minister's presence at the palace. The messenger found the minister in his bath. This state of affairs created a huge uproar. There was no question that the minister had to remain at home and could not come to the palace. The messenger went back to the king for instructions. The king sent a message: "The king commands you to complete your bath, and forbids you to go out today. . . . He orders you to expect him tomorrow in your nightshirt, your leggings, your slippers and your night-cap, so that you come to no harm as a result of your recent bath."

GETTING "CAUGHT SHORT"

SEVENTEENTH-CENTURY LONDON DID contain a few, a very few, public toilets, and these were generally open holes suspended from bridges, over the rivers and canals that meandered through London. But it was uncommon for a person to find a public privy very easily. What did a person traveling in a carriage through a neighborhood of London do if he or she were "caught short" (a euphemism for having to go)? Most men simply hopped out and used out-of-the-way street corners. Ladies might duck into an inn or the home of an acquaintance and use a chamber pot there.

A man named Samuel Pepys had a friend do just that in 1665, and he wrote about the incident in his diary. Lady Sandwich must have been passing by his home when she was "caught short." Most likely, a servant would have answered the door and probably sent word to Samuel that he had a visitor. Samuel rushed home to greet her and found her sitting on a potty in his dining room. The two made awkward conversation while she sat on the chamber pot. You wonder what became of the servant.

PLAGUE AND PESTILENCE

THE BLACK DEATH CAME to overcrowded, unsanitary London in the early spring of 1665. Because of crop failures the year before, hungry rats may have moved into the city, lodging in the poor neighborhoods and bringing diseased fleas with them. A long dry spell meant that the piles of waste heaped up around the streets did not wash away, and the rats thrived.

People living in slums got the disease first. They died with shocking suddenness. The living dragged their dead out of doors and dumped them in the street. Huge plague pits were dug, and bodies were carried there and dumped by men desperate enough to take on that grim job. Death carts piled with corpses rattled through the empty streets. Although firm figures are hard to determine, London's population before the plague had probably been about four hundred thousand. Less than a year later, as many as one hundred thousand people may have died.

THE
Dreadful Visitation:
IN A
SHORT ACCOUNT
OF THE
PROGRESS AND EFFECTS
OF THE
PLAGUE,
The last Time it spread in the City
of LONDON, in the Year 1665;
EXTRACTED
From the MEMOIRS of a PERSON who
resided there during the whole Time of
that INFECTION:
WITH
Some Thoughts on the Advantage which would
result to Christianity, if a Spirit of Impartiality
and true Charity was suffered to preside amongst
the several religious Denominations, &c.

DEUTERON. Chap. XXXII. 29.
O that they were wise, that they understood this, that
they would consider their latter End.

PHILADELPHIA:
Printed by HENRY MILLER, in Second-Street,
M DCC LXVII.

Dreadful visitations by the plague were all too familiar to seventeenth-century city dwellers.

Although no one had yet definitely linked the cause to the fleas on the rats that fed on the general filth, people were slowly starting to realize that there was a connection. One of the early theories was that the plague was being spread by cats and dogs. So the mayor of London came up with what we now know to be an ill-advised decision: he ordered the extermination of all the cats and dogs. Unfortunately, the result of killing all the cats—natural predators of rats—was that the rat population was able to multiply, causing the plague to spread.

In France, the plague broke out in one place or another nearly every year of the seventeenth century, and city officials made similar misguided decisions. When plague struck Lyons in 1628, people who tried to flee were stopped by neighboring townspeople and forced back inside the city walls. In many towns, no one was allowed to enter, or to exit, houses where plague had struck. People had to dictate their wills at the top of their lungs from upper stories of their houses.

A doctor in Marseilles, France, during an outbreak of plague.

THE GREAT FIRE

BY AUTUMN, THE PLAGUE deaths in London finally started to diminish, possibly because the flea population was dying out with the colder weather. But then another disaster struck the beleaguered city. Early one morning in 1666, in a bakery on Pudding Lane, a fire started. It spread quickly, devouring the old wooden row houses that had been built so closely together.

The Great Fire raged for five days and engulfed huge parts of London. Frantic residents dug up the streets and broke open the old wooden pipes to get at the water to try to extinguish the flames. The resulting water stoppages all through the city caused more buildings to be consumed by the fire. As much as 80 percent of the city was destroyed. Amazingly, only five deaths were recorded, although the actual number may have been higher.

THE AFTERMATH

THE DOUBLE-WHAMMY OF plague and fire left mid-seventeenth-century Londoners reeling. But the fire may have inadvertently saved a lot of lives. It destroyed large areas of unsanitary housing and killed off the disease-carrying rats. By about 1700, the city had been mostly rebuilt in brick and stone, and the old, narrow, medieval quarters were replaced with wider, cleaner streets in many neighborhoods. Catastrophic disease would not strike London again for almost two hundred years, with the arrival of cholera in the nineteenth century.

FUN FOR ALL AGES

PUBLIC EXECUTIONS, A MAJOR form of entertainment for all ages, added to the stench of the town. Corpses were often cut into quarters and the bits and pieces were nailed up in various parts of the city, where they were left to rot. (Heads were usually mounted over the city gates to greet visitors.)

Not his real hair.

LOUIS THE P-U-EEY

IN 1643, A FIVE-YEAR-OLD CHILD became king of France. His name was Louis (pronounced "LOU-ee") XIV. Standing at five feet, four inches, this rather short king ruled for a very long time—seventy-two years. (He died in 1715.) He was not short on ego, though. He called himself the Sun King *(le roi soleil)* and considered himself ordained by God to rule over France. To celebrate his own grandeur, he built a gigantic, ornately decorated palace, which was larger than most towns of the period. He called it Versailles (pronounced "vair-SYE") and packed it with every aristocrat in the land.

WHAT DID FRENCH COURTIERS USE FOR TOILET PAPER?

SOME USED SOFT CLOTH, such as silk or linen. Some used a handful of goose feathers. But because feathers didn't provide the necessary leverage needed to wipe one's behind, some people went a step further. They left the feathers attached to the neck of a dead goose—and used that.

NOT ENOUGH CLOSESTOOLS, NOT ENOUGH BATHING

AT THE ROYAL COURT of Versailles, there were seven hundred rooms and five hundred hunting hounds but only about 275 closestools. Since there were at least twenty thousand people living at the palace, well, you can do the math. People relieved themselves anywhere and everywhere. The glittering corridors, rooms, and courtyards reeked of both pet and human excrement. French people of the seventeenth century shared with the British an aversion to immersing themselves in water. They also covered their bodies down to the wrists with heavy, unventilated clothing. As a result, the courtiers, who bathed about once a year, probably smelled worse than the palace did.

The active, amorous, athletic King Louis was bathed only twice in his adult life, both times for medical reasons. The royal bath caused a lot of concern, as nearly everyone believed that bathing allowed bad germs to invade the body through the pores. Many precautions were taken in the days leading up to the bath, including purging and enemas to prevent excessive water from entering the king's body.

Just don't look behind one of those pillars.

The king established a complicated system of etiquette that his courtiers were required to follow. The idea behind it was that they would be so busy following the rules, they would have no time to plot against him. For instance, no person could turn his back on a member of the royal family, or even on a picture of one of them. People had to walk out of rooms backward. They had to bow before the king's bed, even if he wasn't in it. Dozens of courtiers vied for the privilege of being present in the royal bedchamber to witness the king's elaborate morning and evening rituals, which included the privilege of being in the king's presence for his royal BM. The king had two "gentlemen of the bedchamber," who wore black velvet and who had the honor of emptying the royal chamber pot. He often received visitors while seated on his closestool, which secretly appalled many of them.

People actually *wanted* this job!

After Louis's death, doctors discovered that the king's stomach was twice the size of that of an average person, as was the length of his intestines, which may have explained his enormous appetite and the unusually long time he spent seated on his closestool.

HOW DID THEY KNOW HOW BIG LOUIS XIV'S STOMACH WAS?

TOO MUCH INFORMATION?

TMI

AFTER A MEMBER OF the royal family died, doctors immediately performed a postmortem, which is an examination to see how the person died. This process meant carving open the newly dead person on the spot. Grieving relatives had to stand and watch while the gruesome examination was conducted.

· 9 ·

All Dressed Up but Nowhere to Go

THE SCIENTIFIC REVOLUTION AND THE AGE OF ENLIGHTENMENT

AS THE 1700S APPROACHED, many of the old ways of thinking began to change. A scientific revolution was unfolding. New machines were invented. Great thinkers began identifying the laws of the physical world. Newton, for example, watched an apple fall and sought to understand gravity. (The apple may or may not have bonked him

on the head.) Even deeply religious scientists believed that reason, more than prayer, would reshape the world. Perceptions of God changed. He was described as "God the Watchmaker," a metaphor that reflected the new understanding of an orderly universe. And fittingly enough, it was a watchmaker who finally invented a flushing toilet, in 1775.

But in spite of all the amazing new inventions, the water that was available to seventeenth-century city dwellers grew ever more stinking, disease-ridden, and polluted. No one in their right mind considered drinking it.

It wasn't until the 1820s that really powerful microscopes were developed. Cells weren't acknowledged as the basic units of life until the 1830s. As a result, people of the eighteenth century weren't yet focusing—literally—on disease-causing pathogens in the water supply. So, what *did* people drink?

PICK YOUR POISON

YOU'D THINK IF THE only water you had to drink was that foul, you'd find a way to clean it up. But no. The eighteenth-century person's solution—like his Renaissance predecessors'—was to drink alcohol. (A little later in the century, the English also started to drink a lot of tea—see the next chapter.)

EQUINE DINING

NOMADS OF CENTRAL ASIA, who spent huge amounts of time on horseback, came up with a creative solution for slaking their thirst. During times when water could not be found, they would slit open a vein on their horse's neck and drink some of the horse's blood.

TMI · TOO MUCH INFORMATION?

BLACKBEARD

EVEN PIRATES, WHO WERE used to roughing it, didn't like drinking the filthy water they stored on their ships. To help mask the taste, they mixed the water with rum and called it grog. Not surprisingly, most pirates were nearly always drunk.

Blackbeard, whose real name was Edward Teach (or Tache or Thatch), was one of the most feared pirates of the eighteenth century. His favorite drink was rum mixed with gunpowder. He was fond of setting it on fire before drinking it.

Mind if I smoke?

CASTLE MANIA

SAD SLOPPY WEATHER.

Watch where you're walking!

EUROPE AND ENGLAND DOMINATED most of the world during the 1700s. European and British ships sailed to Africa's coastal regions, intent on colonizing them. England ruled over India. It was a period characterized by land-grabbing, absolute monarchs. Many European rulers in particular seemed to feel a need to express their power by erecting grandiose architectural monuments to themselves.

But these monarchs left out a rather critical planning detail. No one bothered to improve the situation at ground level, let alone *below* ground level. Elegant palaces stood next to sprawling slums, where the poor lived in cramped, rat-infested hovels. The most splendid-looking cities—Paris, Venice, Berlin, St. Petersburg—had streets and canals that were filthy and

Potty humor circa 1783.

Monsieur, be so obliging as to make kiss with us.

By the House of Bourbon. With the war we'll go on.

stank horribly. Street drainage was faulty or nonexistent. There were no traffic laws. Chickens, pigs, and herds of livestock wandered among lowly horse carts and fine carriages. (The city of Berlin could be smelled six miles away.) As for conditions belowground, no monarch made an effort to build new sewer systems or to improve the few that existed.

As the century unfolded, radical notions began to arise, questioning absolute monarchy and asserting that people—ordinary people—should have some say in the way they are governed. Did the filth in the cities contribute to these radical ideas? You could certainly make that argument. So what was it like to live in a city in the eighteenth century?

FORCED LABORER

Forced laborers built St. Petersburg, Russia, for Peter the Great (1672–1725), a Russian czar who stood nearly six foot eight. St. Petersburg became the new capital of Russia in 1712. Often referred to as the "Venice of the North," St. Petersburg typified eighteenth-century city building. Its wide boulevards, enormous palaces, and gracious buildings were constructed on the marshy swampland at the mouth of the River Neva, with little thought given to accompanying them with a decent sewer system. And building the city was miserable work. It took twenty years of toil by peasants and convicts, who often tried to run away. Deserters who were caught had their nostrils sliced. As many as thirty thousand of them died from malaria, dysentery, and sheer exhaustion. As a result, St. Petersburg is known as the city "built upon bones."

SWELLING AND SMELLING

MORE AND MORE PEOPLE were moving from the countryside to town. Some of the largest cities by the end of the 1700s were Peking, Edo (later renamed Tokyo), Constantinople, and Paris. London was different from these cities because its population was decimated by plague and fire, and its country's form of parliamentary government set it apart, at least somewhat, from many other countries of the time.

Over in the American colonies, the population of cities was dinky in comparison to those of large European cities. In the year 1700, Boston was the biggest city, with 7,000 people. New York (5,000) and Philadelphia (4,400) were next, with Charles Town (now Charleston) running a distant fourth (approximately 1,200 people). Baltimore had fewer than fifty houses in 1752. By 1760, the population of New York City had grown to about 21,000 people.

THE POWDER ROOM

Don't sneeze!

IN SPITE OF WHAT it means today, this room was not a place in which to relieve oneself in the eighteenth century. The powder room was, in fact, a room where you applied powder. Wealthier people on both sides of the Atlantic wore wigs. To wear a wig properly, it had to be oiled and then powdered by your servants. Once the wig was oiled, you stepped into the powder room, having first covered your clothes with a special drape and hidden your face with a paper cone. Then a servant would puff flour over your head with a bellows so that your wig-hair turned snow white. Eventually, wigs were replaced by natural hair, but the powdering continued.

VENICE: MELODIOUS BUT MALODOROUS

VENICE WAS ONE OF the grander cities of the 1700s, but the canals were reeking, the streets filthy. In the city's concert halls, where the music of Vivaldi, Handel, Bach, and Mozart was being played, there were no bathroom facilities at all. People simply relieved themselves wherever they wanted. Imagine what the concert hall must have smelled like after a three-hour performance.

JAPAN AND CHINA—PAYING FOR POOP

LEST YOU THINK EVERY large city in the eighteenth century was one big midden heap, there were some cities in Japan and China that did a better job managing their waste disposal.

Edo may have been the most populous city in the world during the eighteenth century, inhabited by approximately one million people in 1700, in contrast with London's 575,000. Several other Japanese cities, including Kyoto and Osaka, had populations in the hundreds of thousands. In China, Peking was nearly as large as

KIMONO NO-NO?

HOW DID A JAPANESE noblewoman wearing twelve layers of kimonos answer nature's call? A servant placed a T-shaped wooden post behind a box. Then the servant draped the layers of kimono over the post to allow the woman to squat over the box.

You hope for her sake it's not an emergency.

Edo, and, until British imperialists showed up several decades into the century, the people of Peking seemed to enjoy a fairly decent standard of sanitary living. How did the Chinese and Japanese leaders of these huge cities deal with *their* poop problems?

Edo's water-supply system was on a scale that might be compared to the Romans' in size and sophistication. Aqueducts carried the water from nearby rivers. In Japan and China, human waste was considered a valuable fertilizer for crops. Unlike in cities in the West, where people were paid to cart away household waste, in cities in the East, poop was considered so valuable that night soil was purchased with silver. In Osaka, the rights to the poop from the residents of a building belonged to the building's owner. The rights to the urine belonged to the tenants. Selling the stuff was extremely profitable.

As elsewhere, residents of Edo had to work up a sweat lugging water in order to take a bath.

In Edo, human poop was carefully collected, loaded onto ships, and carried to nearby farms, where it was spread on crops. Kyoto and Peking had similar collection procedures. The smell at the wharves as manure was loaded onto boats must have been horrific. But the drinking water stayed cleaner, and fewer people died of disease.

Edo's system was so well designed that when it was modernized at the end of the nineteenth century, the only major change they made was to replace the wooden pipes with metal ones.

A city's water source is always a gathering place, as demonstrated by these residents of Shanghai.

REVOLUTION AND THOSE PESKY COLONIES

OVER IN THE NEW WORLD, certain colonial leaders were among the first to try putting new ways of governing into practice. They began to demand the right to govern themselves. Our founding fathers may have had a lot of bright ideas about the sovereignty of the people, but they didn't do much to improve sanitation. (Ben Franklin was an exception—see below.)

Colonial America's leaders also disapproved of bathing. They shared Europeans' beliefs about bathwater being unhealthy for the body. But they took piousness to a whole new level, believing that soaking naked in a tub might lead to impure thoughts. Laws were passed in a number of colonies that limited or banned bathing.

HYGIENE HEROES

Ben's Bright Ideas
BENJAMIN FRANKLIN

Benjamin Franklin was well known for his practice of taking "air baths." He believed a cold-water bath was too much of a shock to the system, so he advocated cold air instead. He took an air bath every morning, stripping naked in a cool room.

Appalled by the mounds of garbage piling up on the streets of Philadelphia, Ben Franklin established the first American street-cleaning system in 1757. After his death, his will provided money to the city of Philadelphia to build freshwater pipelines. He was one of the first to recognize the probable link between bad water and disease.

WELL, I DECLARE!

WHAT DID THE SIGNERS of the Declaration of Independence do when they had to go, back in 1776? Many of them might have owned "easy chairs." Today, "easy chair" is a term used to describe a comfortably upholstered armchair. But back then, easy chairs almost always included a removable cushioned seat, beneath which a chamber pot was placed, in order "to do one's ease."

Men's fashions of the 1780s called for very tight breeches, so tight that the wearer couldn't even sit down. Men took to ordering two pairs: one for stand-up, formal occasions and the other for everyday wear.

Standing up for his rights because he couldn't sit down?

FRANCE, JUST BEFORE THE REVOLUTION

THE REVOLUTIONARY RUMBLINGS AMONG the peasant classes in France alarmed despotic rulers everywhere. Did the squalor, disease, and piles of poop in French towns and cities bring on the French Revolution? They may have helped speed things along.

Versailles—the palace built by Louis XIV back in the last century—continued to dominate the life of the French nobility for much of the eighteenth century. To support the lavish lifestyle at court, money was drained from the French treasury—money that

And you thought the 1980s cornered the market on Big Hair . . .

came primarily from heavily taxing the peasants. King Louis XVI and his wife, Marie Antoinette, upheld the traditions at court that had been established by the king's grandfather. They continued to insist that their courtiers obey absurdly complicated rules and wear ridiculously elaborate clothing.

Meanwhile, the unfair economic conditions that existed in France for 96 percent of the population were getting worse and worse. Since anyone with money or influence lived at Versailles, which was about fifteen miles from Paris, very little money, time, or energy was spent fixing Paris's faulty drainage and crumbling sewer systems. The already frightful sanitation problems of Paris grew worse rapidly.

In 1789, the peasants revolted, and the French Revolution began.

WHAT NOT TO WEAR IN PRE-REVOLUTIONARY FRANCE

AS IF THE FASHIONS for powdered wigs and absurdly elaborate hairdos weren't bad enough, hooped petticoats came back in style during the mid-1700s. (Remember the farthingales of the Renaissance? See page 64.) Women walked around wearing these covered birdcages, called *panniers*, which were flat in front and back but could be as wide as eight feet from side to side. Doorways had to be widened, special chairs invented, and personal maids enlisted to assist the wearer whenever "nature called." Movement was severely restricted, so servants and laboring people did everything. So how *did* one pee while wearing all that stuff? As one historian describes it, "Until the early nineteenth century [women] wore long dresses and no drawers so it was simply a matter of standing astride some sort of gutter and gazing dreamily about for a minute or so." On other occasions, a lady's maid was expected to shove a large sponge under her mistress's skirts. No wonder there was a revolution.

By the time the French Revolution and the Reign of Terror rolled around, it was better to dress simply if you wanted to keep your own head from rolling around.

Extreme Fashionista

· 10 ·
Eighteenth-Century England: Flushing Away Troubles

ENGLAND STOOD APART FROM its European, Russian, Chinese, and Japanese counterparts for a few important reasons. First, its system of government, a constitutional monarchy, somewhat limited the power of the king. Castle building was practically nonexistent in England in the eighteenth century. Second, many of the innovations in industries enabled a sizable portion of England's population to prosper during the first part of the century. A wealthy middle class arose. But before very long, urban populations began to grow and catch up with increased production.

No one knows for sure how many people lived in London, but some estimate that by midcentury there were about 650,000 people, outstripping Cairo, Constantinople, and Peking. By the end of the century, London had over one million people, in spite of the increasingly unhealthy living conditions. London's death rate was much higher than its birth rate, which would lead you to expect that the population would diminish. But quite the opposite happened; its population increased rapidly, a fact that can be explained only by a constant influx of new people moving to the city from the countryside. What was it like to actually live there?

GETTING AROUND LONDON

AS THE POPULATION OF eighteenth-century London swelled with more and more people, many streets became practically impassable, thanks to the deep muddy ruts, piles of refuse and manure, and dead animals. Since it rained nearly every other day—it still does—you can imagine how muddy things got.

A large carriage could not easily get from one part of the city to another. But for a well-dressed person, walking was unthinkable. Clothes were too valuable, and too difficult to launder, to risk being splattered with the mud and manure of the streets. So, how *did* wealthy people travel through filthy streets that were too narrow for a carriage, without muddying their clothes?

They used sedan chairs.

A sedan chair looked like an old-fashioned phone booth and was large enough to carry just one person. The compartment had holes on either side that could be threaded through by wooden rails, which were gripped by "chair men," one in front and one behind. The rails were long and springy, so the passenger experienced quite a bit of bouncing. And the chair men traveled fast. They outpaced most pedestrians, who were expected to dive out of the way when a chair came bearing down on them.

An early sunroof.

One Frenchman was knocked down four different times, possibly because he didn't understand the chair men's warning shout of "By your leave, sir!"

As city streets became better paved, sedan chairs were gradually replaced by rickshaws in many countries. A rickshaw is a cart with two wheels, pulled by a human driver.

CHAIR MAN

Being a **chair man** was a dangerous job. In addition to the weight he had to carry, there were frequent collisions and incidents of road rage. It must have been especially difficult to be the back guy—you ran more or less blindly, while your partner in the front made sudden dodges, turns, or stops. And you had no way of anticipating what you were about to step in, jump over, or slosh through.

STINKY FLEET!

THE FLEET RIVER RAN through London and had been a dumping place for centuries. The river flooded frequently. During one awful storm, cascading water swept away several houses. Drownings happened often. People would fall into the river and then sink rapidly in the treacherous slime.

To make room for more buildings, the river was covered in several stages over the course of the century, but decaying waste below the paved-over river often exploded. Today the Fleet River still runs underground, beneath what is now Fleet Street and Farringdon Road.

In 1846, a buildup of gases from the covered-over Fleet River caused a huge explosion, destroying three poorhouses and bathing the neighborhood in sewage. Nowadays ventilation systems have been installed.

SINKHOLES

FOR CENTURIES, PEOPLE WHOSE cesspools were overflowing called the night-soil men to empty them. The night-soil men then carted the waste out of town and sold it to farmers, a practice that had been in existence since medieval times. But as London grew larger, its boundaries swallowed up more and more farmland. With farms ever farther away, it became more expensive to hire cesspit cleaners willing to cart the night soil longer distances. So many households simply had the old cesspits covered over, and new ones would be dug.

London at the time still had dozens of creeks and small rivers running through the city, many of which ended up flowing into the Thames. Since so many households and industries began dumping their waste into these waterways, they became terribly polluted. Moreover, the rapidly growing population meant new housing was urgently needed, so many of these small waterways were covered over in order to create more places to slap up hastily constructed housing. No reliable maps existed that indicated where these abandoned cesspits, creeks, canals, and streams had once been. As a result, cave-ins often occurred without notice. When this happened in the street, drivers, carts, and passengers could be swallowed up in an instant. This was an especially ghastly way to die, in a time when there were a lot of ghastly ways to die.

HOME SWEET HOME—NOT

LONDONERS OF THE EIGHTEENTH CENTURY mistrusted bathing, and they didn't much like outdoor air, either. Understandably enough, they believed that the air wafting in from the foul-smelling streets was unhealthy. So they kept their windows tightly closed at nighttime to keep the bad outside air from coming inside. And because landlords were taxed according to how many windows their buildings had, many windows were sealed shut permanently, which did not help the ventilation situation.

But the problem was, indoor air often proved to be a lot deadlier than outdoor air. The nauseating stench in many homes was not just unpleasant—it killed people on a regular basis. Newspaper accounts and reports from the Sanitary Commission frequently chronicled people found dead in their beds, asphyxiated by poisonous "night air" or "sewer gases"—methane and hydrogen sulfide, most likely, the by-products of decaying waste, which probably leaked into people's homes from old cesspits.

CUPPA TEA?

ALMOST NOBODY DRANK TEA in Britain at the beginning of the eighteenth century, but thanks to China's new willingness to open trade routes with the West, nearly everyone did by the end of it. As the century progressed, the cost of tea fell and became an increasingly common beverage for even working-class people. Tea probably saved a lot of lives. For one thing, boiling the water would have killed many germs. For another, tea happens to contain healthful components that ward off many diseases.

LONDONERS ARE FALLING DOWN

BUT AS EVER—AND this can't come as any shock to you by now—without any clean water, many Londoners simply chose to drink alcoholic beverages. On balance, it was probably a much healthier lifestyle choice for the average worker to drink beer or ale rather than the water—and a mild state of constant intoxication was better than dying of a deadly disease. But living in a more or less continuous state of mild intoxication is one thing. Drinking yourself into insensibility is quite another—and that's what a lot of people did when a new beverage arrived on the scene.

FROM BOTTOMS UP TO ROCK BOTTOM: THE GIN CRAZE

DURING THE FIRST PART of the 1700s, an epidemic of gin drinking swept through England. Gin was cheap, reasonably tasty, and highly intoxicating. It quickly became even cheaper as more and more people made and sold it illegally. It was soon being sold on nearly every London street corner. By the 1730s, gin drinking among the poor had reached epidemic proportions, and an increasingly alarmed Parliament passed a series of Gin Acts, trying to stop the epidemic by raising the tax on gin and limiting its sale. Men, women, and children were tossing it back in staggering quantities. Night-soil men

THE RIVAL FOUNTAINS.

OR

GIN AND WATER.

Gin was certainly bad for you—but water wasn't much better.

were routinely rewarded with a bottle of gin as a tip after shoveling out a homeowner's cesspit. In poorhouses, nurses gave it to babies to quiet them, which often worked far too effectively. In 1751, *nine thousand children* died of alcohol poisoning from drinking gin.

There's no doubt that the gin epidemic resulted in many people dying of drink. But malnutrition, disease, dirty food, bad hygiene, and unhealthy water still killed more babies than gin did. Forty percent of all deaths in London during the first half of the eighteenth century were children under two years old.

THE SWIRL HEARD ROUND THE WORLD

IT'S HARDLY SURPRISING THAT toilets were invented—or reinvented—in England. London contained a sizable population of wealthy, middle-class homeowners who sought comfort at levels previously enjoyed only by the aristocracy. In 1775 (the same year the American Revolutionary War began), a British watchmaker named Alexander Cummings filed the first patent ever for a water closet. He figured out how to minimize some of the smells by using something called a U-bend trap. He wasn't laughed out of court the way Harington had been. People seemed ready at last.

But the first toilets weren't all they'd been cracked up to be. They leaked constantly. They also smelled. Sewer gases filled people's homes. Cummings hadn't worked out how to vent the gases properly. Sewer gas, or "night air," as it was called, was highly flammable. The last thing you want to do around flammable gases is light a match, but of course, electricity had not been invented yet. If you rely on candles and fires for light and warmth, you can imagine the consequences of having a home filled with flammable gas. Explosions happened frequently.

Improvements were just around the corner. A few years later, Joseph Bramah improved on Cummings's design. By the turn of the century, over six thousand wealthy English homes had water closets installed. But as a result, further disasters were to unfold.

· 11 ·

The Early 1800s: The Great Unwashed Move to Town

THE PRICE OF PROGRESS

DURING THE FIRST HALF of the nineteenth century, a lot happened in a hurry. To fully appreciate what was going on, it helps to understand more about the major historical period at the time, which came to be called the Industrial Revolution.

YOU SAY YOU WANT A REVOLUTION?

THANKS TO ALL THE discoveries made during the last century, new technologies and machines were invented, or greatly improved, during the early 1800s. These scientific discoveries were not uniquely English or European—in fact, many ideas came from China, India, and other parts of the subcontinent, thanks to newly expanded trade routes. But London was the epicenter of the Industrial Revolution, so it's where we'll focus.

Many newly invented machines could perform the work of several men and did not need to eat or sleep. As a result, a lot of craftsmen and laborers suddenly lost their jobs. Because so many workers found themselves unemployed, employers knew that they could get away with paying very low wages. If one worker protested that he could not

Fewer men, more machines.

feed his family for so little money, the employer knew there were plenty of others who would readily take the job.

Meanwhile, huge numbers of people continued to stream into the larger towns and cities in the hope of finding jobs in the newly built factories and industries. Many found work but for low wages. Many did not find work but stayed anyway. And all those people had to find places to live in a hurry, nowhere more urgently than in London.

THERE GOES THE NEIGHBORHOOD

IN THE FIRST THIRTY YEARS of the nineteenth century, London's population *doubled*. By midcentury nearly three million people were packed into its urban center. By the year 1900, it was the largest city in the world, with nearly 6.5 million residents.

Although London was the biggest city in the world, the same kind of rapid expansion was happening in other cities. Paris had half a million people in 1800. By 1900 it had 3.3 million.

The galloping growth of cities caused big problems for city governments. There just weren't enough places for all those people to live. And there were no systems for getting rid of all the waste they produced. It was the first time in history that so many people had lived so closely together. As cities somehow absorbed more and more—and more—people, the poop kept piling up.

SNORTING SCAVENGERS

WHO WERE THE FIRST garbage collectors? Pigs. Since medieval times, pigs had been wandering the streets in most towns and cities, devouring a lot of the organic material people had discarded, including food scraps and excrement. While they did help get rid of some of the waste, they left their own manure behind.

Pigs roamed the streets of London, Paris, and New York well into the nineteenth century.

The original garbage collectors.

LONDON'S UNDERWORLD

AS LONDON GREW AND GREW, a new "underclass" of unskilled workers emerged. They figured out a way to survive through an unusual combination of creativity and desperation. They made their living by scavenging and recycling the enormous amounts of waste generated by all those densely packed city residents. Some of the jobs they performed had existed for centuries, while others were peculiar to the nineteenth century and had odd-sounding names. The night-soil men who shoveled out cesspits replaced the medieval gongfermors, and the dustmen collected household garbage. There were also toshers, mudlarks, pure collectors, rag and bone collectors, and catgut makers. All of these workers labored in a world filled with garbage and excrement.

The reasonably well-paid night-soil men occupied a place in this world that was just on the fringe of respectability. Emptying cesspits was a pretty disgusting job, but people realized it was a necessary one. "Respectable" people viewed most of the other jobs with loathing. And yet, in a society with no organized system of waste management, these workers performed a vital role.

ICKY OCCUPATIONS

PURE COLLECTOR

Next time your mom asks you to empty the garbage, don't complain. After all, things could be a lot worse. You could have been a nineteenth-century **pure collector**.

"Pure" was a euphemism for dog poop. Collecting pure was usually performed by children. They walked all over the city, scooping up dog doo with their bare hands (easier to clean than gloves, after all). Tanners paid as much as a shilling a bucket for the dog doo. They mixed it with urine to soften leather.

LONDON'S ROOKERIES

SO WHERE DID ALL these teeming masses of newly arrived laborers from the countryside end up? Most crammed into neighborhoods in London's East End. Shoddy housing was hastily constructed alongside existing houses originally built for a single family but now packed with multiple families. These slums came to be known as "rookeries." Ramshackle buildings teetered over stinking canals and unpaved lanes too narrow to qualify as streets. These neighborhoods were never cleaned, and there were no toilets in any of the houses. If an animal died, it tended to rot where it lay. Does this description remind you of what you read in the medieval chapters? It was worse, in many ways, because there were so many more people.

Without toilets then, where did people relieve themselves? Most had no choice but to use back alleys as toilets or as places to dump chamber pots. The stench of the rookeries, especially in hot weather, was so overpowering that newcomers often retched and vomited.

A winter evening near a London rookery.

POOR HOMES

YOU'D THINK THAT SHODDY housing, situated in terrible slums, would at least be inexpensive, but it wasn't. Since there were no buses or subways, working people had to live in walking distance of their place of employment. As a result, laborers' families had to live in the central parts of the city. Greedy landlords took advantage of this by charging these people high rents. Whole families squeezed into subdivided dwellings, sometimes with six-foot ceilings, and most often consisting of only one room, without a sink, a stove, or a toilet.

To earn a few extra pennies, families sometimes rented out a spot on their floor where a stranger might sleep. Many one-room apartments were so dreadfully overcrowded that people had to sleep in shifts. People from the countryside often tried to live as they had in the country, and they brought their livestock into their homes to live with them. Possibly the worst places to live were in basement apartments. Sewage frequently flooded basement homes.

THE SWEET SMELL OF SUCCESS

IN NINETEENTH-CENTURY LONDON, you could *see* the difference between rich people and poor people. Rich people didn't just live longer, eat better, and wear nicer clothes. They were usually taller, with straighter backs and limbs. Many poor children suffered from rickets, a disease caused by bad nutrition and lack of sunlight. The disease caused their growth to slow and their bones to curve. A modern-day fifth grader might stand eye to eye with a working adult from a poor London neighborhood of the 1820s.

But what really separated the classes was the way people smelled. The poorer you were, the worse your body, clothes, home, and neighborhood smelled.

Handkerchiefs: don't leave home without one.

No wonder it was so difficult for a poor person to "better himself" or to "rise above his station." You couldn't get a respectable job if no one could stand the smell of you. The shortage of clean water, the high cost of soap, and the lack of spare clothes help to explain why London's poor became known as the "Great Unwashed."

When the railroad companies began transporting passengers in 1825, they tried to keep "workingmen" off the trains because they smelled so bad. Churches actually discouraged poor people from attending.

The worse poor people smelled, the more richer people avoided them. The rift widened between the unwashed classes of people and those who could afford to wash. Many Londoners who lived above the poverty line convinced themselves that poor people *preferred* being dirty and smelly. More than a few writers at the time suggested that the smells, filth, and diseases that plagued poor neighborhoods didn't come from desperate overcrowding and poverty. People *chose* to live that way. Poor people were not just grubby and smelly—they were also thought to be immoral.

Rickets affected many nineteenth-century urban children—and still exists today.

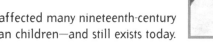

DUSTMAN

Dustmen were nineteenth-century garbage collectors. Many of them picked up more than garbage as we know it; they moonlighted as "night-men," shoveling out cesspits and hauling the waste away in open carts.

Nowadays, nearly everything we buy comes in some sort of package. Back then, shopping bags and plastic wrap did not exist. Households generated a lot less garbage. Still, there was a lot that could be recycled. Dustmen piled household waste onto their carts, then sorted through their horrible-smelling load and resold a lot of it. Ashes went to brick layers, manure to farmers, and dead animals to glue factories, tanners, or catgut makers. Tanners used the skins to make leather. Catgut makers used the intestines of horses and sheep (but not the intestines of cats, despite the name) to make musical instrument strings. Whatever was left over was chucked onto dung heaps or dumped into the river—to be further recycled by the scavengers and mudlarks (see box on page 106).

FASHIONS OF THE TIMES: HOOPSKIRTS

IN THE 1840S, HOOPSKIRTS came back into fashion. These were huge cages made out of thin steel, called crinolines, over which yards and yards of skirt material was draped. The hoopskirt swung like a bell as the wearer walked. It was difficult to sit down modestly while you were wearing the equivalent of a covered wagon.

It's anyone's guess how women in hoopskirts managed to use a chamber pot, but many of the skirts could collapse into a more or less flat "disc" when the wearer sat down. And women were used to practicing the "virtue of control." Just as your parents urge you to use the bathroom before a long car trip, most women knew enough to use the toilet before putting on their large cagelike hoops.

Heavy Metal

MIASMA THEORY

PEOPLE OF THE NINETEENTH CENTURY were used to bad smells. They also believed that bad smells caused disease.

The idea that bad smells, known as "miasmas" back then, cause disease had been around since ancient times. But for centuries, the miasma theory had competed with other equally misguided notions about the causes of illness—things like bodily humors going haywire, evil spirits messing with innocent victims, or, that old reliable explanation, God's wrath. But by the early part of the nineteenth century, as the light in most cities grew murkier and murkier, and the air smellier and smellier, the miasma theory became the *predominant* explanation for what caused diseases.

We know now that the miasma theory was based on flawed logic. People came down with diseases not because the air around them smelled (although it certainly did), but because the air contained germs passed along by an infected person, or, more often, because they drank water or ate food or somehow came in contact with human feces that contained microscopic disease-causing microbes.

Although the miasma theory was eventually proven to be incorrect, it did focus people's attention on the horrible conditions many people were living in, and it sparked a huge new movement devoted to public health.

But the widespread acceptance of the miasma theory caused big trouble, too. One unfortunate consequence was that poor people were blamed for their problems. Their "bad habits" (which stemmed from their unwillingness to keep themselves clean) were making them sick. Another downside to the theory was that many doctors didn't see the point of washing their hands before treating patients. After all, if diseases were transmitted by breathing poisonous air, why bother washing your hands?

14 CROSSING SWEEPER

Crossing sweepers stationed themselves at busy street crossings and earned tips by sweeping the muck out of the way so a fine lady or gentleman wouldn't get dirty. And there was plenty of muck to sweep—over a hundred thousand horses clomped through the streets of London. Each horse dropped about thirty pounds of manure a day. At really treacherous crossings, sweepers might lay down a plank that allowed pedestrians to cross the street. In Paris these crossers were known as *pontonniers volants*. Since many streets had a gutter running down the center, often overflowing with filth, these planks must have come in handy.

ICKY OCCUPATIONS

BUT POSSIBLY THE WORST consequence of all, from a public health perspective, was that most of the people who were in charge of cleaning up the cities were miasmatists. They thought it was more important to eliminate smells in the air than it was to keep the waterways clean. So more and more, the waste removed from city streets was just dumped into the rivers. As a result, the already-polluted rivers that supplied drinking water to people living in big cities such as London, New York, Paris, and St. Petersburg became even *more* polluted.

15 ICKY OCCUPATIONS

SCAVENGER AND MUDLARK

Anything left over by the dustmen was further recycled by scavengers. **Scavengers** crawled around on the dung heaps, searching for valuables that had been thrown away by accident. As you can imagine, this must not have been a very high-yield job, since the dustmen would have already combed through it.

Mudlarks were scavengers who searched for valuables by wading into the putrid muck along the riverbank at low tide. They were very often children. Mudlarks worked barefooted, searching for lumps of coal, rusty nails, bits of rope, anything that could be sold for pennies. Besides being freezing work, it was highly dangerous. A cut foot could—and frequently did—become infected rapidly, often resulting in death.

· 12 ·

Vileness in the Victorian Era

THE VICTORIAN ERA

Queen Victoria and her beloved husband, Albert.

QUEEN VICTORIA ASCENDED THE throne in 1837, at the age of eighteen. She went on to reign a whopping sixty-four years, until her death in 1901. People often use the phrase "Victorian Era" to describe the whole of the nineteenth century, which isn't technically true.

TOILETS AND THE TROUBLES THEY CAUSED

WE'VE BEEN WAITING OVER a hundred pages for real, flushing toilets to show up. So why, now that they've at long last made an appearance in this toilet chronicle, did they get a mere passing mention two chapters ago? After all, you may be thinking to yourself, weren't flush toilets the engineering marvel that civilization had been waiting for?

Well, here's the ironic twist: early toilets turned out to be weapons of mass destruction.

As more and more people began to install WCs, many of London's streets got noticeably cleaner. The problem was, the toilets flushed waste into the old, outdated sewers and on into the Thames. The combined efforts of the miasmatists and people who installed flushing toilets led to a rapid and horrific contamination of the Thames. Remember, Londoners *drank* this water. Although accurate statistics are impossible to calculate,

New toilets made the streets look cleaner while the water became dirtier.

it's safe to say that the miasmatists and the toilet-flushers unwittingly helped to send thousands and thousands of people to an early grave.

AT FIRST, INTO THE CESSPITS

AT FIRST, THE NEW toilets were simply hooked up to private cesspits. You can imagine the result. If you attach a water balloon onto the end of your garden hose and turn the water to a tiny trickle, you can fill the balloon and have time to tie it off. But if you turn the tap to a gush, the balloon fills way too fast and bursts quickly.

By the same principle, most cesspits, overloaded to begin with, couldn't handle it when gallons and gallons of extra water and waste were suddenly flushed into them. They tended to quickly and catastrophically overflow. And in the jammed neighborhoods of London, cesspits and drinking wells could be situated dangerously close together. When the cesspit overflowed, the sewage mixed with the drinking water. And as we know by now, it's a bad idea to drink water that is laced with sewage.

This disastrous overflow problem wasn't limited to London. It happened in city after city during the nineteenth century as cities everywhere developed and grew. As soon as running water became available, but before any sewers were built, huge numbers of wealthy city dwellers began installing toilets. In Boston, in 1864, there were over fourteen thousand water closets. In Buffalo, in 1874, there were over three thousand in use.

AND THEN, INTO THE SEWERS

LONDON HOMEOWNERS QUICKLY GREW tired of clogged pipes and overflowing cesspits. So they started hooking up their WCs directly to the city's ancient, crumbling drains. And suddenly the waste from thousands and thousands of homes began pouring into the river.

This sudden influx of excrement was a catastrophe for the city's drinking water. By 1850, the Thames had become a giant cesspit—for three million people.

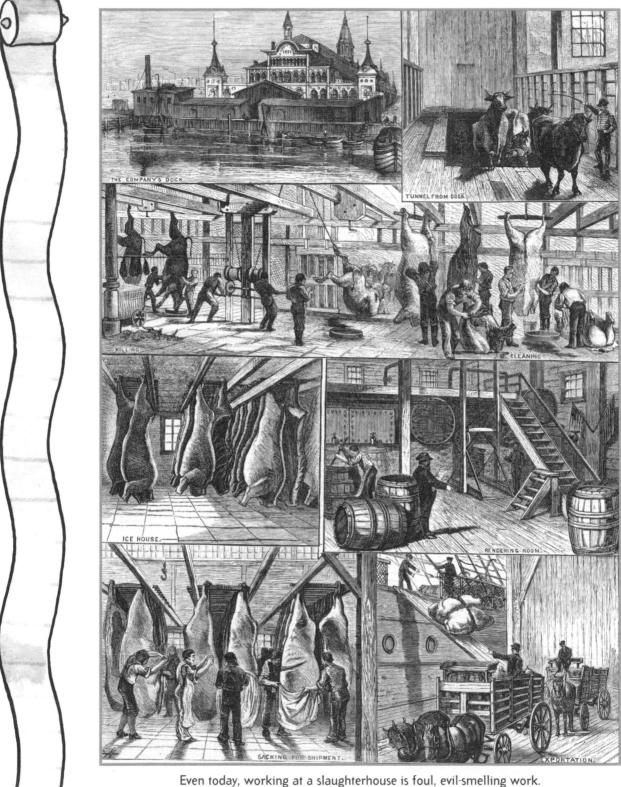

THE COMPANY'S DOCK

TUNNEL FROM DOCK

KILLING

CLEANING

ICE HOUSE.

RENDERING ROOM.

SACKING FOR SHIPMENT.

EXPORTATION.

Even today, working at a slaughterhouse is foul, evil-smelling work.
In nineteenth-century cities, slaughterhouses were a major contributor to pollution.

RENDERER

16 ICKY OCCUPATIONS

What became of all those dead horses, dogs, and pigs, not to mention the remains of slaughtered animals at the slaughterhouses? London, New York, Paris, and other big cities began to enlist the service of rendering companies. Like so many others in the scavenging underworld of nineteenth-century cities, **renderers** (also called knackers) realized that money could be made from recycling—and their product was animal carcasses. Renderers would collect dead animals and wheel them off to the factory, which was often, though not always, at the outskirts of the city. The animal carcasses and offal (bits and pieces from slaughterhouses) were boiled in huge vats of water and made into things like gelatin and glue. The bones were ground up to be used as plant fertilizer. Just imagine what the air smelled like when the stench of boiling rotten carcasses mixed with all the other stenches in the air.

OTHER UGGY INDUSTRIES

TO MAKE MATTERS WORSE, all those booming new industries were dumping *their* waste products into the Thames. Animal carcasses from slaughterhouses and chemicals from industries tumbled into the river alongside dead horses, dogs, cats—even murder victims. Everything was dumped, poured, and heaved into the river. Poisonous gases burbled and popped on the greasy, oozy surface. Boaters started getting sick. Fish disappeared. The only creatures that seemed able to survive in the reeking muck were eels. Coincidentally, eels became a very popular street food.

MMM-MMM!

NOWADAYS, HEALTH EXPERTS CAUTION people against
eating eels caught in polluted waterways. But
back then, most people had larger health concerns
to worry about.

Eels have long been an inexpensive form of
protein in many countries. Jellied eels and eel pies
are still popular menu items in many eateries in
East London today. Be sure to try some if you travel
there.

Hot eel soup for sale!
Unless you prefer them cold and jellied.

DON'T DRINK THE WATER

EIGHT PRIVATE WATER COMPANIES supplied drinking water to Londoners, and it was a
profitable business. The quality of the water they supplied to their customers varied
tremendously around the city. At some street pumps, the water came out cooler and
clearer-looking than at others. At some, it tasted salty, the result of the Thames being a
tidal river that mixed with the ocean into which it flowed. Five of the water companies
made no effort to filter their water—on several occasions, live eels came wriggling out
of people's water pipes. Worse still, several of the water companies drew their water
downstream of the city, where the river was most polluted.

By the mid-nineteenth century, profit-greedy private water companies controlled the
flow of water from the river, and they tended to give preferential treatment to customers
who were able to pay. In many working-class London neighborhoods, water flowed from
the neighborhood standpipe for only an hour a day, three times a week, and never on

Sundays. Imagine how long the lines must have been. When families ran out of water, they often dipped their pots into the nearest polluted river or canal. In one crowded neighborhood, the water was turned on between 4:35 a.m. and 4:55 a.m. *only*. In another, a riot occurred when the water ran for only five minutes.

Even the royal family couldn't escape the smelly Thames.

AND DON'T BREATHE THE AIR

EVEN THE QUEEN HERSELF had to deal with sewage problems. Queen Victoria and the rest of the royal family lived in Windsor Castle, which had been built right on the banks of the Thames. When heavy rains caused the river to overflow onto the palace lawns, raw sewage remained behind, and the air reeked. The sewage had to be raked back into the river. During dry spells, the sewage just lay along the banks of the river. It smelled so disgusting, parts of the castle could not be used.

CLOP-CLOP, PLOP-PLOP

IT'S POSSIBLE YOU MAY have met people who claim that we ought to go back to the time of the horse and buggy. These people will try to convince you that the days before cars were invented were simpler, cleaner, more wholesome times. Don't listen to these people.

In the dreadfully overpopulated urban centers in the nineteenth century, the traffic jams, noises, and, worst of all, piles of manure generated by horses were serious and very smelly problems. In dry weather, the droppings dried up and were ground into dust, which swirled into people's clothes, hair, and eyes with every passing carriage or cart. In wet weather, the droppings mixed with all the other mud in the streets and turned everything to stinking muck. Street cleaning did occur in wealthier neighborhoods, but the piles of manure and other waste were usually just carted to poor neighborhoods and dumped there. Towering piles of horse (and human) manure often grew to the size of small houses.

If tramping through the streets was tough on pedestrians, it wasn't much fun for horses, either. The average life expectancy for a horse in New York City in the mid-nineteenth century was about two years. (Modern draft horses generally live to be twenty to twenty-five years old.) Horses often slipped on the slick cobblestones and broke a leg, and would then have to be destroyed on the spot. Others just keeled over and died from overwork. In 1880, New York City officials removed fifteen thousand dead horses from the streets.

A dead horse lying in the middle of the road could be a big problem in a busy part of town. If you've ever tried to lift a thirteen-hundred-pound horse, you will understand why people usually didn't bother trying. In poor neighborhoods, they simply left the animal carcass to rot. When animals dropped dead in better neighborhoods, people called the renderers (see page 111).

Like most people, most work horses lived short, miserable lives.

GOODY GOODY GUMDROPS

TOO MUCH INFORMATION? **TMI**

HAVE YOU EVER WONDERED WHAT HAPPENS TO LARGE FARM animals when they die? Or that dead deer by the side of the road? Or the bits and pieces left over at slaughterhouses? Quite often, the remains are sent to rendering plants. It's a quiet but enormous industry that you don't hear much about. In a process that is too disgusting to describe—which is saying something in a book such as this—the animal carcasses are rendered, and the resulting product is then filtered, refined, and turned into things like gelatin, lipstick, cement, polish, candles, and gummy candies. (Think about *that* the next time you're swapping Halloween candy with your friends.) The heavier "material" gets dried out and ground up and made into pet food and livestock feed.

Gumdrop? No thanks.

· 13 ·

Cholera: The Disease That Changed the World

THE MOST DREADED DISEASE

HORRIFIC AND INCURABLE DISEASES were a way of life—and an all-too-common way of death—for people of the nineteenth century. But cholera inspired a particular horror.

Cholera gets an entire chapter in this book because it fundamentally altered the world and compelled world leaders, whether they liked it or not, to change the way they governed. Rulers realized they had to leave off building grandiose monuments to themselves and begin constructing invisible but essential infrastructure instead. They *had* to—it was a matter of life and death, potentially *their* lives and *their* deaths. Within fifty years of cholera's arrival, most major world cities

People tried all kinds of clothing and devices to ward off cholera.

began building new sewer systems. (Those that didn't suffered ongoing catastrophic outbreaks of the disease.)

Cholera is an ancient disease, but prior to the nineteenth century, it had been seen only in India and the Asian subcontinent (countries south of the Himalayas). Still, people in the West knew about it and feared it.

In 1817, the disease began to spread. It traveled from Asia to Russia, the Middle East, and the Ottoman Empire. And then, in 1832, it roared into England and Wales. That year it killed eighteen thousand Londoners, mostly poor people living in crowded slums. The same year it carried off twenty thousand Parisians, and then it crossed the Atlantic to Quebec and Montreal by way of ships carrying infected passengers.

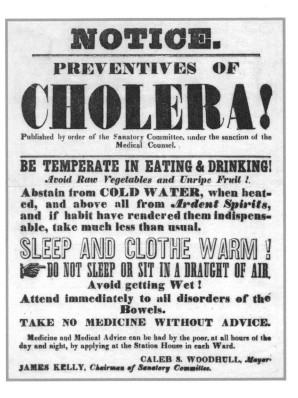

New Yorkers had been tracking cholera's path with dread. Once in America, it killed thirty-five hundred New Yorkers before spreading westward.

Cholera was an awful way to die.

A GHASTLY WAY TO GO

CHOLERA, WE KNOW NOW, is a disease you catch if you somehow swallow a single-celled microscopic bacteria known as *Vibrio cholerae*. It is a highly contagious disease, but it is not spread through the air. Cholera microbes live in water that has been contaminated by the feces of an infected person. In other words, you catch cholera by drinking dirty water. But back in the 1830s and 1840s, people did not know how the disease was transmitted. The miasma theory still prevailed, so people thought you caught it by breathing air containing poisonous miasmas.

Once they have been ingested, the cholera microbes lodge in a person's intestines. There they multiply quickly. They block the body's ability to absorb water, and cause the victim to expel enormous quantities of fluids (through vomiting and diarrhea) in a

QUARANTINED CHILDREN OF CHOLERA VICTIM

Cholera victims were often quarantined (kept apart from other people).

shockingly short amount of time. Bucketfuls of excreta were dumped into gutters, back alleys, and cesspits. When the contaminated waste seeped into wells or other sources of drinking water, the disease spread quickly and easily.

Part of the horror of cholera was that it struck its victims so quickly and so ferociously. Stories circulated about people who felt fine one moment but then pitched forward face-first into the street, as though they'd been hit over the head, only to be dead in a matter of hours.

Usually, the disease lingered for several agonizing days. The first stage of diarrhea would be followed by vomiting and insatiable thirst. As victims rapidly lost fluids, their eyes would grow sunken. Their skin turned leathery, and their body would be racked with agonizing cramps. The heartbeat dropped, oxygen levels lowered, and the victim turned a ghastly shade of blue. Soon after that the victim usually died.

WHAT—OR WHO—KILLED TCHAIKOVSKY?

HERE'S WHAT WE KNOW: Peter Ilyich Tchaikovsky, a famous Russian composer, died of cholera in 1893. He contracted the disease after drinking a glass of unboiled, contaminated water.

Here's what we don't know: Was he forced to drink it, by people who wanted him dead? Did he drink it on purpose, to commit suicide? Or was it purely accidental? The idea that it was an accident seems unlikely; by then everyone knew that water was unsafe to drink. Some scholars have suggested that he was murdered, forced to drink the contaminated water by a secret Russian court to cover up his affair with a young Russian nobleman. Others think he wanted to kill himself, because he was distraught by the unenthusiastic reception his latest symphony had received. We may never know the true story.

THE EFFECTS OF CHOLERA: CHADWICK AND THE CLEANLINESS MOVEMENTS

IN 1842, EDWIN CHADWICK, a well-known British social reformer, published an account about the sanitary conditions of working people. It became famous instantly. In his report, Chadwick asserted that more urban dwellers died from filth and bad ventilation than had died "in all the wars the country has been engaged in in modern times."

In 1848, Chadwick was appointed Sanitation Commissioner. His sanitation reform movement swept through England. Chadwick caused enormous improvements to be

Edwin Chadwick—he meant well, anyway.

made throughout England's cities. He ordered street cleaning, sewer flushing, cesspool emptying, and carting away of dung.

Cities across the globe—many of which were reeling from cholera epidemics of their own, and also from bloody revolutions—followed Chadwick's example. They created their own sanitary movements. Maybe, city officials reasoned, well-scrubbed streets would not only reduce the chances of another cholera epidemic, but they would also produce happier citizens, less prone to revolt in the future. Modern cities owe a big debt to Chadwick. Thanks to him, a new type of centralized city government emerged, one that accepted responsibility for improving public health.

The problem with Chadwick's thinking—and the reason that he isn't one of our Hygiene Heroes—is that he was a staunch miasmatist. While he worked overtime to prevent cholera by reducing the "noxious vapors" in the air, the actual source of the disease, the reeking Thames, was becoming a giant vat of cholera-laden soup—thanks to more and more flushing toilets and ever-more street filth getting dumped into the water.

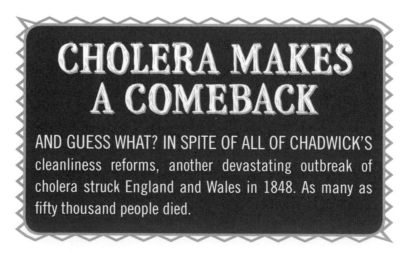

CHOLERA MAKES A COMEBACK

AND GUESS WHAT? IN SPITE OF ALL OF CHADWICK'S cleanliness reforms, another devastating outbreak of cholera struck England and Wales in 1848. As many as fifty thousand people died.

THE BROAD STREET PUMP

IN 1849, SOON AFTER that devastating outbreak, Dr. John Snow published a paper in which he proposed a radical theory: cholera, he asserted, is spread through the water and not through the air. If cholera were caused by miasmas, Snow reasoned, why didn't people constantly exposed to bad-smelling air—like sewer workers, for instance—fall ill with cholera more regularly than others? (They didn't.) And if it were something breathed in, then why didn't the disease attack the lungs? (It didn't—it attacked the intestinal tract.) The river, he claimed, was the true source of the disease. But all his evidence was circumstantial. He had no proof.

The water pump—
the main source of water . . .
and disease.

Snow's theory met with a great deal of resistance. Practically everyone at the time was firmly convinced that cholera was spread by poisonous miasmas.

In 1854, Snow had a chance to test his theory. Another terrible cholera epidemic raged through London. It would eventually kill thirty thousand Londoners. In one section of the city—in fact, Snow's own neighborhood—a baby fell ill with what was thought to be diarrhea. Her mother soaked the baby's soiled diapers and dumped the bucket of dirty water into the building's leaky cesspit. The baby's illness turned out to be cholera, which proceeded within days to kill hundreds of people in the neighborhood. Snow noticed that people who drank water from the Broad Street pump—the standpipe nearest to the sick baby's house—were developing cholera. Yet people living just across the street from the pump, in the Poland Street workhouse, were not getting sick at all. Nor were workers at the nearby Lion Brewery. If the cause were actually bad air, Snow reasoned, shouldn't the nearby brewery workers and the wretched workhouse inhabitants fall ill as well?

As it turned out, the workers at the brewery received ale as part of their wages, so they drank that instead of water. Residents of the workhouse did not drink Broad Street well water either, because the workhouse happened to have its own well.

Snow persuaded city officials to examine the drains. Sure enough, crumbling brickwork was found beneath the street, allowing the sewage from the leaking cesspit to mix with the drinking water in the well. Still far from convinced that Snow was right, but desperate to try anything, officials ordered the handle of the Broad Street pump removed. But by that point everyone in the neighborhood had either died or fled, so it still wasn't clear if Snow was right or wrong. But it was a start, and his work steered scientists away from miasmas and got them to start examining the water.

HYGIENE HEROES

The Microbe Hunter
JOHN SNOW

Dr. John Snow was the first person to assert that cholera was spread through the water, not through the air. It took ten more years before Snow's theory was accepted by the medical community. Unfortunately, Snow died before his theory could be proven. By the 1870s, Louis Pasteur would go on to prove the existence of disease-causing microbes. In 1883, a German scientist was finally able to isolate the cholera microbe and prove its existence. But Snow's work had paved the way for a new science: microbiology. And it also forced cities to confront the hard truth about the state of their water supply.

· 14 ·
The Revolting River

ENOUGH IS ENOUGH

BY THE MID-1800S, it had finally dawned on people that poor sanitation was posing a threat to everyone's health. It was hard not to arrive at this conclusion, what with people dropping dead by the tens of thousands. What had been seen as an inevitable part of urban living—stinking streets, sickly children, and dreadful diseases—finally crossed the line of tolerability. People demanded action. The question was, what do we do now?

THE GREAT EXHIBITION

IN 1851, BRITAIN PUT on a display called "The Great Exhibition of the Works of all Nations." The Crystal Palace, an enormous structure made of glass and iron, was built in London's Hyde Park to house the exhibition. Between May and October, more than six million visitors came to see the exhibition. An inventor named George Jennings installed "retiring rooms and washrooms," complete with flushing toilets, which could be used by the public for a penny (men could use the urinals for free). Over the course of the exhibition, more than eight hundred thousand people "spent a penny" in Mr. Jennings's "halting stations."

The Crystal Palace—site of the first public flush toilets.

What's perhaps most striking is the fact that prior to this time, public restrooms *hadn't existed* in theaters, stadiums, and other large gathering places. Imagine yourself attending a sporting event at a stadium, for several hours, with ten thousand other people, and having *no access to a bathroom*. It's practically unfathomable to us nowadays.

AND THE GAME GOES INTO OVERTIME!

The newfangled flushing toilets gave people firsthand experience with the strange contraptions, and they must have liked what they saw. More and more middle-class homeowners installed toilets. By 1857, there were two hundred thousand flushing toilets throughout London. And all drains led to the river.

THE BIG STINK

IN THE SUMMER OF 1858, there was a long dry spell, followed by a terrible heat wave. For two weeks in June, the Thames began to smell really, really bad. Victorian noses were used to tolerating awful smells, but this was a new low. There was no escaping it. The Thames smelled so vile that the British Parliament, which met in buildings right along the river, could not meet. The drapes of Parliament were soaked in chloride of lime in an unsuccessful effort to keep out the smell. Huge amounts of lime were dumped into the water. But nothing helped.

Because its water level was low due to the drought, the river could not push the sewage out to sea. When the tide came in, the sewage would simply get pushed back upstream. The excrement of three million people remained in the shallow water, baking in the heat. The newspaper headlines screamed, THE THAMES STINKS! People actually vomited from the stench.

The Thames at its all time smelliest.

In addition to being disgusted, people must also have been totally terrified. Remember, most people were still convinced that diseases were caused by poisonous miasmas in the air. Members of Parliament acted uncharacteristically quickly. They passed new antistink laws in a record-breaking eighteen days. Included in their panicked legislation was the approval of the construction of a massive new sewer system. Luckily for them, a young engineer had joined the Sanitary Commission as assistant engineer a few years earlier and then had been promoted to chief engineer when his boss died. His name was Joseph Bazalgette.

BAILED OUT BY BAZALGETTE

BAZALGETTE (1819–1891) **BECAME** an instant hero, enjoying rock-star status. His sewer-building project was the most ambitious engineering feat of the nineteenth century. Bazalgette built huge brick tunnels beneath the city, including one that ran right beneath the Thames; hundreds of workers were employed and not a single man died.

Bazalgette built pumping stations to drain low-lying areas and created wide embankments along the river, which narrowed and deepened the river and freed up large amounts of land in the crowded city for new buildings.

Bazalgette's new sewers emptied London's sewage into the river well east of the city, many miles farther downstream. This did wonders for London's drinking water. But as you might expect, it didn't go over quite so well with the towns downstream, which suddenly began receiving London's wastewater. It wasn't until the end of the nineteenth century that London built wastewater treatment plants and stopped dumping untreated waste into the waterways.

In 1864, a salmon was spotted swimming in the Thames, something not seen since the days of Henry VIII.

Bazalgette's embankments vastly improved the look—and the smell—of the river and its surrounding areas.

HYGIENE HEROES

The Great Preventer
JOSEPH BAZALGETTE

Joseph Bazalgette's eighty-two miles of sewers transformed the Thames from the filthiest urban river in the world to one of the cleanest. Thanks to his work, virtually every major city in the world began to work on establishing a sanitary-water system and a well-functioning waste-removal system by the turn of the century. Bazalgette was knighted in 1874.

Although it's impossible to measure specific numbers, it's safe to say that together, Joseph Bazalgette and John Snow saved thousands and thousands of lives by preventing future epidemics from occurring. They're probably two of the most important people you've never heard of.

A London rat catcher—the Verminator!

THE DEFEAT OF THE DISEASE

THE YEAR 1866 SAW London's very last cholera epidemic. By then, most of London was connected to Bazalgette's sewer network—all but the East End, a notoriously poor section of the city. It was the East End neighborhoods that were ravaged by the disease.

Cities in India that were ruled by the British did not benefit from improved infrastructure. In Bombay and Calcutta, the British installed modern plumbing for its officers but not for the rest of

the population. So cholera epidemics happened frequently, long after they had been eradicated in Britain.

Cholera epidemics still occur, even in this day and age. Epidemics tend to strike in developing countries where poor sanitation is still a big problem. But nowadays cholera is curable if treated at an early stage.

17 ICKY OCCUPATIONS

TOSHER

Toshers were people who searched for "treasure" down in London's sewers. Toshers sloshed though mile after mile of sewage-laden water, in dim lighting, sorting through the muck for coins and other trinkets that may have been accidentally dropped and washed into the street drains. It was dangerous work. They risked deadly attacks by vicious rats, sudden cave-ins, poisonous gases, and explosions.

· 15 ·

The Age of Plumbers

NEW TOILETS

NEW TOILETS WERE BEING designed. New sewage systems were being built. Someone needed to figure out how everything worked. Enter the Victorian plumber.

Now that sewer systems existed, toilets began to make a lot more sense. Toilets were not invented in one fell swoop. Inventors continually tinkered and refined the designs by Cummings and Bramah, gradually improving them in stages.

Victorian toilets were ornately designed, full of curlicue motifs and frou-frou details. Most of the early toilet makers were artists and pottery makers. Royal Doulton, which was (and still is) a company well known for creating fine china, made some of the first toilets. Another Victorian toilet designer, Thomas Twyford, was originally a pottery maker specializing in teapot design. He went on to design some lovely, decorative ceramic toilets that looked suspiciously like teapots. His company still exists today.

Toilet-like teapot, or teapot-like toilet?

The Flushing Toilet vs. The Earth Closet

A FAD?

THE NEW TOILETS WERE still viewed warily by many people. A lot of people considered the new flushing toilets just a fad, and a bad fad at that.

THE EARTH CLOSET

FOR THOSE WHO FEARED having sewer gases roiling around their homes, an inventor named Henry Moule introduced a contraption called the Earth Closet in 1860. Like a giant litter box, the Earth Closet used earth rather than water to combat odors. The user would turn a crank after using the toilet and fine, dry earth would be dropped onto the waste in the basin. The Earth Closet had a lot to be said for it. It was simple to repair and easy to clean, and since it used no water, it did not add to the overflowing household cesspit or the river-polluting sewers. The downside was that the earth had to be emptied, usually by a housewife or servant. Moule sold a lot of his Earth Closets, which tells you how suspiciously the first WCs were received by the middle class.

TOILET TIMELINE

1596 Sir John Harington invents the flush toilet for himself and Queen Elizabeth.

1775 Alexander Cummings reintroduces the flush toilet.

1788 Locksmith Joseph Bramah further refines the design. But the sound of the flush is deafening, and toilets often clog and break.

1852 George Jennings improves the design even more and molds toilets into fancy shapes.

1857 An American engineer named Julius Adams lays twenty square miles of pipes in Brooklyn and publishes his technique, which allows engineers in other cities to use his designs as a model.

1860 Henry Moule introduces his Earth Closet.

1865 Joseph Bazalgette completes the bulk of his London sewer-building project.

1884 Thomas Crapper adds a few more refinements to the toilet, including the pull chain and automatically filled bowl.

1885 Thomas Twyford makes the toilet all one piece, eliminating leaks.

1904 Thomas Crapper retires from his plumbing business and sells it to his partners, who run the company well into the twentieth century. The name "Crapper" appears on many of the company's toilets. During World War I, U.S. soldiers in England see the name "Crapper" on toilets and begin referring to the toilet as "the crapper."

1907 The flushometer is invented, which uses pressure rather than gravity to flush.

1900–1932 The U.S. Patent Office receives applications for 350 new water closet designs. In a change from the highly decorative Victorian designs, twentieth-century toilets are much sleeker and simpler in their design. Now that toilets are within reach of more and more people, mass production becomes more important than artistic expression. By this time, engineering companies have taken over toilet production from the pottery makers, and these engineers are more interested in function than form.

1991 The U.S. Congress makes it illegal to dump sludge (the solids from a wastewater treatment plant) at sea.

1992 The U.S. Congress passes a law that requires all new toilets to be designed with a 1.6-gallon flush rather than the 5 to 7 gallons they used to use. (The Japanese have had them since the early 1970s.) These "new" toilets save a lot of water.

2004 A high-tech toilet is launched with a heated seat that opens automatically when the user approaches, a front-and-back warm-water spray to wash the user's behind, and a power catalytic air deodorizer. The toilet even "knows" what days and times it is typically not used and powers down its warming coils to conserve energy.

2015 The United Nations pledges to cut in half the number of people without access to a flushing toilet by this date.

THE PLUMBERS

WITH THE HEROIC DEFEAT of cholera and the dawning understanding that microbes, not evil air, caused many diseases, plumbers and sanitary engineers became the heroes of their day. In the 1870s, plumbing was still a dangerous profession. It was quite possible for a plumber to die in the line of duty, by explosions or poisoned gas.

Plumbers were still learning how toilets worked. Early toilets had no valve traps to keep the sewer gases from backing up into people's homes. Many families had them installed underneath their stairs, with no ventilation at all.

A lot of plumbers and sanitation workers were injured or killed in explosions from buildups of methane and other gases. Others got sick from diseases. Many plumbers carried a small bottle of peppermint oil to homes where pipes were leaking. A leak could be traced by adding a drop or two of peppermint oil into the pipes at the top of

Early plumbers, Victorian heroes.

the house and then sniffing the pipes for a minty smell, which would tell the plumber where the leak was. The peppermint oil was powerful stuff. Just a drop could be smelled from quite a distance.

In addition to using their noses on the job, plumbers also relied on rats. A dead rat was an indication that poisonous sewer gases might be present.

Queen Victoria's husband, Prince Albert, died of what was probably typhoid

TRAUMATIC TRAIN TRAVEL

DURING THE 1870S, WCs WERE INSTALLED IN train cars for first-class passengers for the first time. It wasn't until 1880 that third-class passenger cars had WCs installed.

in 1861, and ten years later their son Edward nearly died of typhoid as well. He, his friend, and his groom all caught the disease while staying at a house in the country. The groom and the friend died, but Edward survived. A plumber traced the source of that disease to a leaking cesspit and fixed it, further cementing plumbers' heroic status in Victorian society.

HYGIENE HEROES

You have probably heard the name Thomas Crapper, and you may even have heard that Crapper invented the toilet. Not true. Crapper was certainly a talented plumber. In fact, he was a royal sanitary engineer, installing bidets and urinals in the homes of the royal family. He was also an important inventor. During his career Crapper filed for nine different patents, all plumbing related. But he has to share the credit with the rest of the toilet inventors.

The Flap About Crapper
THOMAS CRAPPER

PARIS SEWERS

PEOPLE IN OTHER CITIES, terrified of cholera, had been watching the events in London and realized that sewers were not just nice to have—they were a matter of life and death.

In Paris, construction began in 1852 on a magnificent sewer system. Designed by Eugene Belguard, the sewers were the pride of Parisians. By the 1860s they started conducting tours through them. Lords and ladies in their nicest finery were taken through the tunnels on boats. To be a Paris sewer man became a legitimate and even respectable profession.

But because the Seine was slower moving than the Thames and had less water in it, some engineers predicted that there would not be enough pressure in the sewer pipes,

The ultimate log-flume ride!

or a strong enough current in the river, to move waste toward the ocean. Ignoring these warnings, and fed up with cesspits and night-soil collectors, Parisians began dumping all their household filth and garbage into the sewers. Using special boats, the sewer men pushed the sludge through the new sewers and out into the river.

As it turned out, the engineers were right. The Seine did not have enough water to dilute all the filth, nor was the current fast enough to wash it out to sea. The stinking mass of sewage moved along close to the banks without mixing into the rest of the river. The sewage did not freeze in the winter, and in summer ominous gas bubbles burbled and broke at the surface.

In 1880, Paris experienced its own Big Stink.

THE FRENCH BIG STINK

DURING A PROLONGED HEAT wave in July, the Seine began giving off a foul stench. Unlike the English stink, which had lasted for about two weeks, this one went on for two months. By this time, microbiologists had proven that many diseases were contracted by drinking polluted water. Yet even so, the French had a harder time figuring out what to do about their reeking river. The great Louis Pasteur proposed building separate sewage systems—one for rainwater runoff and one for waste—and sending the sewage out to sea. Eventually the French passed a law that allowed for the construction of aqueducts and pumping stations that carried the sewage farther away from the city. It wasn't until 1899 that Parisians stopped dumping untreated sewage directly into the Seine.

· 16 ·

Sludge, American Style

COUNTRY FOLK

OUTSIDE OF BIG CITIES, most nineteenth-century Americans still used out-houses (or chamber pots during stormy weather). It was very common for out-houses to have two, three, or more toilet seats in a row, so that more than one person could use them at the same time.

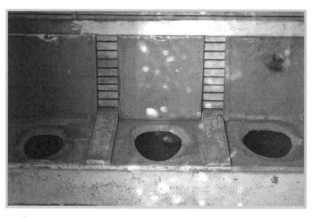

A three-seater outhouse in Connecticut.

CITY FOLK

HUGE NUMBERS OF EUROPEAN immigrants flooded into American port cities during the mid-1800s. Many of these Europeans were driven to leave home by wars, poverty, famine, and religious intolerance. So American city planners had to scramble to figure out where to put people, and of course, where to put their waste, just as their European counterparts had to do a few decades before.

The crumbling sewers were the first to feel the strain of all these new people. Leaky, wooden-log sewer pipes just couldn't handle the waste. American city officials, terrified of cholera, followed the European trend and built brand-new sewer systems.

By midcentury, sewers were laid in Philadelphia, followed by Chicago, Boston, and Washington DC. New York City also began construction, although corrupt city officials slowed the process considerably.

England's flush toilets didn't really catch on in America until the 1870s, and even then they were found only in wealthier homes. Poorer people continued to make do with chamber pots.

MANHATTAN DRINKING WATER

DURING THE EARLY PART of the century, New York had major water problems. Water was not just scarce, but what supplies there were tasted salty and became more and more polluted. In 1829, the city finally built its own reservoir. But the pipes did not reach far enough south to supply water to those living in the slum neighborhoods at the southernmost tip of Manhattan. These residents continued to rely on filthy wells. When cholera tore into town in 1832, the people in these neighborhoods died by the thousands.

At last, in 1842, New York City completed construction on the forty-mile Croton Aqueduct, which piped water from the Croton River into a giant receiving reservoir in what would become Central Park. This new reservoir (which still exists today) could hold 180 million gallons of water and fed into the receiving reservoir at Fifth Avenue and Forty-second Street.

The Croton Reservoir was built on Fifth Avenue, where the New York Public Library now stands.

NEW YORK ABSORBED FAR more immigrants than any other American port city. Its population ballooned during the 1840s. The newcomers were mostly Irish (driven from home by the potato famine) and German (driven from home by the revolution in 1848). Most recent arrivals settled in the southern part of Manhattan, crowding into houses that had been designed for single families. Most of these buildings had no sanitary arrangements at all. Meanwhile, the rich moved north. Many built new mansions along Fifth Avenue.

New York quickly became the filthiest city in America. The sanitation problems in the poor districts grew worse and worse. Mud, garbage, and excrement were heaped up in huge piles. Roving groups of pigs took care of some of the garbage, but most of the rest was left to rot.

Imagine living in a five-story building in a densely packed Manhattan neighborhood, and having to share outdoor privies with as many as twenty other families. In some buildings, these privies were rarely cleaned and constantly clogged. Many people found it a lot easier to steal outside after dark and dump the contents of their chamber pot onto the street. No one would be likely to notice one more pile of dung in the already filthy streets and alleyways.

In lower Manhattan, multiple families often shared outdoor toilets and water standpipes.

Home
sweet
home.

ICKY OCCUPATIONS

NECESSARY TUBMAN

In Manhattan, human excrement was supposed to be stored in privy vaults, big stone containers that needed frequent emptying. The privy vaults were emptied by the American equivalent of night-soil men, workers called **necessary tubmen**. Practically all the tubmen were African American, as it was one of the few occupations available to them.

As late as the 1870s, most apartments in working-class neighborhoods of New York City still had no inside bathrooms. People had to use outdoor toilets, which were usually stinking holes in tiny courtyards, used by multiple families.

THE CIVIL WAR

SANITATION HAS ALWAYS BEEN a big problem for soldiers during wartime, and the American Civil War was no exception. Three of every five soldier deaths were caused by filthy living conditions. Typhoid, diarrhea, and dysentery killed far more soldiers than bullets did.

MUCKRAKING AND MUCK

TOWARD THE END OF the century, the social conscience of middle-class Americans began to awaken at last. Thanks to mass communication—newspapers and magazines—awareness began to increase about the plight of the poor and their appalling living and working conditions. In a study done in New York City, surveyors determined that at least *half* of New York City's population lived in tenements (run-down, overcrowded apartments). The Lower East Side was the worst. Families were packed in more densely than in poor London neighborhoods.

In 1906, President Theodore Roosevelt introduced a new expression to describe journalists who investigated terrible working and living conditions, and who exposed corruption to the public. They became known as *muckrakers*, literally, people who rake manure. Nowadays we know them as investigative reporters.

Rub-a-dub-dub—in a tenement tub!

Nelly Bly may look pretty clean, but she was a muckraking journalist who flung a lot of mud.

HYGIENE HEROES

Washing Away Corruption
GEORGE WARING

In 1894, a man named George Waring was appointed to be the new commander of the Department of Street Cleaning. Waring had helped design sewer systems all over the United States. At the time that he took charge, the department was in a terrible state of disorganization. Snow was never removed from most streets, nor were the 2.5 million pounds of manure that were being deposited each day. Corrupt workers spent most of their workdays in saloons.

Waring, a Civil War colonel, insisted that his two thousand employees wear white uniforms and march in military fashion through the streets. He called them "soldiers of the public," but everyone else called them Waring's "White Wings." Thanks to Waring, New Yorkers began to sort their garbage to be collected. Most of the streets were scoured, and snow was at last shoveled away.

George Waring's White Wings were recognized as New York heroes because of their work cleaning up the city.

HYGIENE HEROES

Cholera Crusader
DR. HERMANN BIGGS

New York had experienced several devastating cholera outbreaks during the nineteenth century, but in 1889 another hero of public health, Dr. Hermann Biggs, started a cholera-prevention movement. Several years before, a terrible outbreak of cholera had struck Germany and Russia, where it killed twenty-five hundred people a day for weeks on end. Biggs established a new policy. If a New York resident fell ill with what was thought to be cholera, the victim was immediately tested. Once a case was confirmed, Biggs's workers scoured and fumigated the victim's lodging, and then burned the clothes and bedding. His army of workers cleaned streets, scrubbed tenements, and flushed out waste pipes. The result of his campaign was that only nine New York City residents died of the disease in 1892.

WASHING UP IN WASHINGTON DC

WOODEN PIPES HAD BEEN installed at the White House way back in 1831, but it's not certain when running water and flushing toilets first made an appearance. Running water probably didn't pour into presidential bathtubs until about 1877, when Rutherford B. Hayes was in the White House. His wife, Lucy—nicknamed Lemonade Lucy because she disapproved of alcoholic beverages in the White

The White House in 1877.

House—is usually credited with having running water installed. Flushing toilets were probably installed at around the same time.

But even after that, the White House continued to have plumbing problems. When President James Garfield was shot in 1881, he was taken back to the White House to recover. After spending several weeks there, his health declined steadily. People blamed the plumbing for the president's failing health. Sewer gases were leaking from the outdated pipes, and the president was moved to his home in New Jersey, where he died two weeks later, eighty days after being shot. Garfield's successor, Chester A. Arthur, refused to move into the White House. He was convinced that the leaky plumbing contributed to his predecessor's death, due to poisonous sewer gases. He tried to get Congress to tear down the White House and build a sewer-gas-free copy in its stead, but though the Senate approved $300,000 for the project, the House of Representatives would not go along with it, and the new president had to settle for an overhaul of the plumbing in the old building.

A colossal tub for a colossal man: William Howard Taft, twenty-seventh president of the United States, needed a special oversized bathtub built to accommodate his 300-pound self.

· 17 ·

Modern Sanitation

THE PROGRESSIVE ERA

YOU HAVE PROBABLY HEARD THE word "progressive" before. It means being in favor of change and improvement, and pretty well sums up the work of many reformers who lived during the early part of the twentieth century. Three presidents called themselves progressives: Theodore (Teddy) Roosevelt, Woodrow Wilson, and William Howard Taft. But Teddy Roosevelt embodied the Progressive movement. Among other things, he passed laws that cleaned up slum housing, sanitation, and drinking water.

By the early 1900s, people had finally begun to notice something important: if you flush raw sewage into the river, terrible diseases occur in the populations of people living downstream. So at long last, cities in both Europe and America

Teddy Roosevelt, getting the crowd excited about reform.

began to install water filtration and chlorination systems. And thanks to Roosevelt, they also built wastewater treatment facilities. Finally, raw sewage stopped getting dumped directly into the waterways.

Party in the sewer!

TWENTIETH-CENTURY TOILETS

IT TOOK A WHILE for flushing toilets to reach most American households. During the 1930s, only *half* of the houses in the United States had indoor plumbing.

A toilet from the 1930s—plain, no-frills— and the style hasn't changed much since then.

GO FOR LAUNCH!

IN 1961, ASTRONAUT ALAN B. SHEPARD JR. lay strapped into his space capsule, waiting to become the first American launched into space. But the launch was delayed for several hours, and Shepard realized with horror that he really, really had to pee. Upon consulting Mission Control, he was told to pee in his space suit. But because of the danger that he would short-circuit all the sensitive electrical equipment inside his suit, they turned off the power while he did so. The mission then proceeded successfully.

Cop a squat.

SIT, STAND, SQUAT

YOU MIGHT BE SURPRISED to find that toilets in different parts of the world can look different from the one you have at home. Throughout history, toilet design has been related to clothing styles. For instance, in cultures where people have worn robes (such as Roman togas or Turkish caftans), toilets tend to be holes in the floor. People just hitch up and gather their garments around the waist, and then squat over the hole. In cultures where people wear pants (or, in the past, leggings or hose), toilets tend to be the sit-down type, since these types of clothing end up bunched around your ankles.

SQUATTERS

SQUAT TOILETS STILL EXIST IN MANY COUNTRIES around the world. Many people consider them a lot more sanitary than our seated models, once you've figured out how to use them.

ACHOO!

GERMS—STILL WITH US

WE'VE COME A LONG way from the miasma theory of disease. Thanks to microbiology, we know that microbes—disease-causing bacteria—lurk everywhere. And yet even in this day and age, many people believe that most illnesses are spread through the air. While it's true that viruses can be spread from person to person through the air by sneezing and coughing, 80 percent of viral infections are spread through hand contact. Many make you sick with diarrhea and painful stomach cramps. Some cold and flu viruses can live on surfaces for up to three days. In developing countries, diarrhea is a leading killer of children in the world (behind pneumonia and acute respiratory infections due to air pollution, and ahead of AIDS and malaria).

ATTENTION: GERMAPHOBES

EVER SINCE PEOPLE HAVE learned about the existence of microbes, they have worried about "catching germs." What are the germiest places in your home? No, not the toilet seat. Ready to get grossed out?

• The germiest places in your home are dishrags, sponges, and cutting boards. In fact, your kitchen sponge is probably brimming with E. coli.

• According to microbiologist Chuck Gerba, if you have to choose between licking your toilet seat and licking the door handle on your refrigerator, choose the toilet.

• When you flush the toilet, a microscopic cloud of germs is released into the air, eventually settling on every surface in a six-foot area around the toilet. And closing the lid doesn't help; the microscopic mist hangs around for two to four hours.

• Outside the home, the keyboard on your school's computer can be a serious ick-zone. So can shopping cart handles, playground equipment, and ATMs.

• In public bathrooms, you're better off drying your hands with a paper towel than using one of those hot-air dryers. Rubbing your hands under the hot-air device actually increases the bacteria flying around the bathroom and increases bacteria on your hands by 162 percent. Paper towels decrease the level by 29 percent.

Does this mean you should walk around wearing rubber gloves all day? That's not practical. The best way to protect yourself from germs is to wash your hands with hot, soapy water for at least 15 to 30 seconds. Or use an alcohol-based hand sanitizer if you can't use soap and water.

HOW DO ASTRONAUTS USE THE TOILET IN SPACE?

If you think about how much gravity matters when you sit on the toilet, you'll appreciate the problems faced by astronauts in a weightless environment. In older spacecrafts, the toilet was little more than a plastic bag taped to the astronaut's behind. But in spacecrafts built more recently, "waste-management systems" have improved a lot. Nowadays, the astronaut straps him- or herself onto a padded toilet seat, which creates a nice "seal" between butt and seat. Male astronauts use a funnel-shaped urinal attached to a suction hose to pee; females use something similar but shaped slightly differently. The astronaut turns on a fan that sucks the waste away from the body and traps it in a bag. It's basically like sitting on top of a big vacuum cleaner. Solid waste gets compressed and then freeze-dried. Then it is stored in an unmanned spaceship and released into space.

Urine is channeled into a different compartment and is periodically released into space, where it immediately vaporizes. Apparently it is a splendid sight. According to one astronaut, "There is nothing as beautiful as a urine dump at sunset."

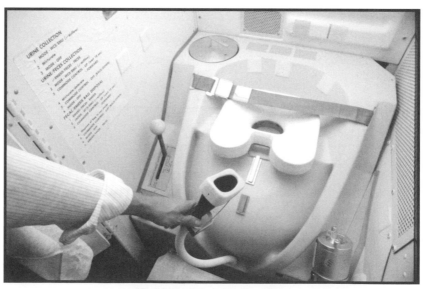

The first space shuttle toilet.

· 18 ·
Toilet Talk

NOW YOU KNOW: it's important to understand your past—including the history of your own toilet—in order to plan for the future.

One thing we've learned the hard way is that managing waste still has a long way to go. Toilets are an engineering marvel, right up there with other amazing inventions, such as the wheel and the telephone. But they're not the perfect solution. Just pushing waste farther away from us isn't a good long-term solution—it's going to come back to haunt us eventually. "Making it go away" by dumping waste into the nearest moving water source can protect people from some diseases in the short term, but it exposes them to other, potentially more serious ones. Nowadays a lot of the world's sewage ends up in the oceans.

URBAN LEGEND

THE *NEW YORK TIMES* reported that on a snowy evening in 1935, several teenagers discovered an eight-foot alligator in a sewer in Harlem. The boys had been shoveling snow and dumping it into a manhole when they spied the half-dead reptile thrashing around ten feet below the street level. After dragging it out with a clothesline, they whacked it over the head with their snow shovels and killed it. The newspaper theorized that the reptile had fallen off a boat passing in the nearby river. But others claimed that lots of reptiles lived in the New York City sewers, possibly from having been flushed down the toilet by parents unwilling to keep them as pets any longer. Most experts agree that there are no longer any alligators, but you never know.

EUPHEMISMS FOR THE TOILET

AMERICANS AREN'T THE ONLY ones who use euphemisms to refer to the toilet. British people use them too, and their words aren't any more precise than ours. For instance, "toilet" derives from the French word *toilette* and was originally used to describe the process of getting dressed. And "water closet" has nothing whatsoever to do with pooping, does it? Here are some other words people have come up with for the toilet, according to bathroom historian Frank Muir:

bog house

closet of ease, stool of ease, or house of easement

comfort station • garderobe

halting station • house of honor

house of the morning

the jakes, or Ajax

the john • latrine • lavatory

the loo (probably English people mispronouncing
the French word *l'eau,* which means "water," or *lieu,* which means "place")

necessary house • powder room • privy

receiving house

reredorter (literally meaning "the room at the rear of the dormitory")

temple, or temple of convenience

throne • water closet (or WC)

le water closet, le wattair, le double (short for W)

pissoir (a French urinal)

the
john

latrine

POLLUTION

THE PRACTICE OF TREATING wastewater at treatment plants before dumping it back into the waterways has been a huge benefit to the planet. But even after it is treated, the water contains a lot of nitrogen and phosphorus—as well as other contaminants like sodium and chemical wastes. Any gardener will tell you that nitrogen and phosphorus are ingredients in most fertilizers, and they help plants grow. Unfortunately, when they enter the water, they cause algae to grow, namely, microscopic organisms called phytoplankton. A surplus of this algae blocks sunlight and pollutes the water. When the algae die, they sink to the bottom, where they get consumed by bacteria—which in turn multiply and use up a lot of oxygen. So the oxygen levels in the water drop, which causes fish and other living things to die.

WATCHING OUR WASTE LINES

GUESS WHAT USES THE most water in your house? Toilets. Followed by showers and baths. That's a lot of water getting wasted. According to the Environmental Protection Agency, thirty-six states are expected to have water shortages over the next ten years. So we need to come up with some water-saving solutions quickly.

TOILET PAPER

TOILET PAPER WAS INVENTED in China in 1391 AD, but you had to be an emperor to be allowed to use it.

Toilet paper for ordinary people was invented by an American, Joseph Gayetty, in 1857, but it did not catch on right away. In the era before supermarkets, you had to ask the grocer for every item you bought, and many nineteenth-century housewives were too embarrassed to ask out loud for toilet paper.

TOILETS OF THE FUTURE

VERY SOON YOU MAY have two options on your toilet. The new "dual flush" models allow you to choose the size of your flush. One button is designed for liquid waste (3 liters per flush), and the other for solids (6 liters per flush). This device saves bucketfuls of water—estimates are that the dual-flush toilets can save nearly twelve thousand gallons (over 45,000 liters) of water per toilet per year. Composting toilets are also gaining in popularity.

Although it may be years before new toilet technologies find their way into your bathroom, you have quite a bit to look forward to. Many already have hands-off flushing devices so you don't have to touch the bacteria-infested toilet flusher. You'll probably see reverse fans and filters that will absorb smells. Some toilets will even be equipped with medical-testing devices, like those that can test the level of blood sugar in your urine.

DIAPERS: A HISTORY

IN TROPICAL CLIMATES BABIES could go around naked, but in colder climates parents (usually mothers) had to figure out how to keep their babies reasonably clean. Since biblical times infants have been wrapped in "swaddling clothes," which varied from place to place but which were basically swaths of absorbent linen or wool wrapped around the baby's bottom.

The Elizabethans didn't change their babies' diapers more than once every few days. Diaper rash must have been a major problem.

In some Native American tribes, mothers packed moss inside rabbit skins to serve as diapers.

In the American West, wet diapers were usually dried in front of the fireplace and then slapped back on the baby—without being washed.

Safety pins were invented in 1849. A rectangular linen or cotton cloth was folded around the baby's bottom and safety-pinned on each side of the baby's waist.

By the twentieth century, many mothers simply threw dirty diapers into a big pot of boiling water. They would then dry them in the sun. This was a lot of work.

The first disposable diapers appeared just after World War II. These diapers, which were called Chux, had padding that resembled paper towels. In 1961, Procter and Gamble applied for a patent for a more sophisticated disposable-diaper design, which they called Pampers.

Diaper services were popular during the 1950s and 1960s. Soiled diapers were collected and replaced with clean ones.

During the 1960s and 1970s, disposable diapers changed and evolved quickly and were no longer luxury items.

Nowadays, 85 to 90 percent of all diapers used in the United States are disposable.

You've come a long way, babies.

THE POOP ON DIAPERS: WHICH ARE BETTER FOR THE ENVIRONMENT, CLOTH OR DISPOSABLE?

UNFORTUNATELY, NO ONE CAN say definitively which are better for the environment. Ask any parent or day-care worker: disposables are extremely convenient. Cloth diapers are a huge pain in the neck. But would Earth be a greener place if parents made the effort?

According to one recent report, if you calculate the energy invested in creating all the disposable diapers that a baby uses in a year, you use up the equivalent of fifty-three gallons of gasoline. That's not a major drain on our nation's resources, if you compare it to the energy that cloth diapers use up getting laundered. The energy required to heat the water plus the effects of the detergent on the environment more or less balance out the equation.

Two other major accusations have been leveled at disposables: First, they fill up the nation's landfills. Second, they pose a threat to public health because they obviously contain poop, which gets chucked into the landfill untreated.

The average baby goes through about five thousand diapers before it is potty trained. And the majority of those diapers are disposable. But disposable diapers make up no more than 2 percent by weight of the average landfill's solid waste contents. (Newspapers and construction materials take up vastly more space.) In other words, eliminating disposable diapers would have very little impact on the state of modern landfills. As far as the threat to public health, landfills are already terribly hazardous places, and the contribution from diapers is a drop in the diaper pail when you consider that 20 percent of the sludge from sewage treatment plants, 8 percent of waste from septic tanks, and untold amounts of medical waste get dumped there too. And no diaper—not even the biodegradable ones now being sold—can break down in a landfill, where there's not enough oxygen for much of anything to decompose.

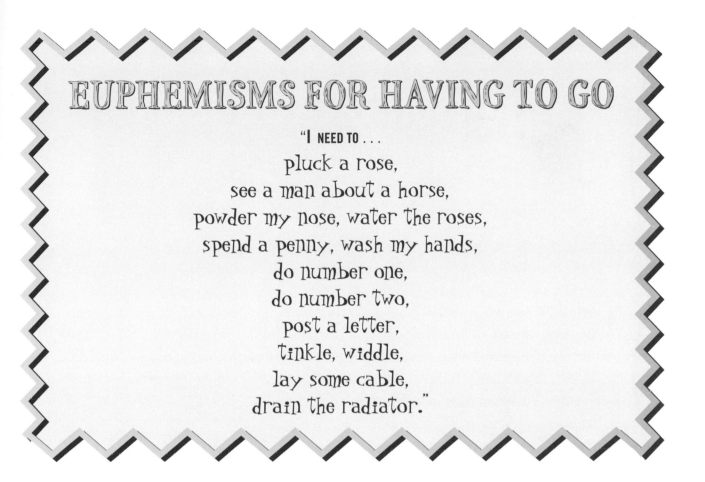

EUPHEMISMS FOR HAVING TO GO

"I NEED TO . . .
pluck a rose,
see a man about a horse,
powder my nose, water the roses,
spend a penny, wash my hands,
do number one,
do number two,
post a letter,
tinkle, widdle,
lay some cable,
drain the radiator."

SANITATION IN THE DEVELOPING WORLD

IMAGINE YOUR LIFE WITHOUT toilets. Then think about this: in 2004, only 232 towns in India had sewer systems, out of a total of 5,003. In India today, about seven hundred million people have nowhere to relieve themselves except outdoors. As a result, the Ganges River, considered sacred by Hindus, is severely contaminated. So is most of India's produce, which is often irrigated with contaminated water. Infant mortality approaches the levels of Victorian England.

A private group called Sulabh has built thousands of public latrines in more than a thousand cities. Some cost as little as $10 each. Users spend two cents to use them, but they are free for children, the disabled, and the poor.

Improving water supplies and sanitation in the developing world is the key to everyone's future.

TOILETS: THE NEW CRADLES OF CIVILIZATION

THINK OF THE AMAZING inventions and discoveries that have occurred in recent history: cars, the theory of relativity, airplanes, televisions, computers. Because of their relative simplicity, and their ubiquity, toilets often get overlooked, but they shouldn't. Toilets, together with modern sewer systems, have made it possible—in fact, actually pleasurable—to live in high-density cities.

Thanks to toilets, modern medicine, and modern sanitation systems, we are now healthier and live longer than ever before in history. But technology has also created new challenges. We've moved our waste farther away from us, out into the oceans, but we haven't figured out how to eliminate it completely. And in the developing world, a lot of people are still unwashed and sick.

According to a UN report about the global water crisis, it would cost $10 billion a year to halve the percentage of people without safe drinking water and to provide them with simple pit latrines. That's less than half of what rich countries spend on bottled water in a year.

But even in countries where advanced sewage systems exist, the problems are increasing. Plumbing needs to advance and change. Our present sewer systems are damaging our waterways. We need to find a way to convert sewage into usable fuel. What's the answer?

There's no simple solution, but one answer is sewage-powered fuel cells. These are being developed by scientists at Penn State University. These fuel cells are sort of futuristic batteries, powered by sewage, that never go dead. They have the potential to be converted into electricity. It's going to take a lot more work and research, but many people believe it's part of the solution that can save our energy-hungry, sewage-laden planet. So pay attention in science class. The world is going to need your help.

Notes on Sources

Chapter One

Steven Johnson, in his excellent book *The Ghost Map: The Story of London's Most Terrifying Epidemic—and How It Changed Science, Cities, and the Modern World* (New York: Penguin/Riverhead, 2006, pages 92–94) was a great resource to me in helping to explain how cities were able to grow so rapidly.

Chapter Two

The seven plagues theory comes from May R. Berenbaum's book *Bugs in the System: Insects and Their Impact on Human Affairs* (Reading, MA: Addison-Wesley, 1995, page 113). According to Berenbaum, flies, lice, and locusts are pretty self-explanatory. Cattle diseases could have been the result of biting flies. Boils could have been caused by buboes/fleas, scabies, or bot flies. Even "darkness" could have been a swarm of locusts darkening the sky. As for the plumbing—"blood" might have been red water, the result of elevated bacteria levels, and "frogs" might have left the water and appeared on land due to the unsanitary state of the water. The point about insects being humankind's worst enemies comes from Berenbaum (page 194), and she also gives a great explanation of how insects act as disease vectors (page 201).

Chapter Three

The dinopoop information comes from an article by R. Monastersky in *Science News* (vol. 153, 20, 25. June 20, 1998), which can be found online at www.sciencenews.org/pages/sn_arc98/6_20_fob2.htm. Much of the information about sanitation in ancient times came from Lawrence Wright's *Clean and Decent: The Unruffled History of the Bathroom and the W.C.* (New York: Penguin, 2005, see in particular pages 10–11), and from Julie Horan's *The Porcelain God: A Social History of the Toilet* (Secaucus, NJ: Carol, 1997, page 4). The Essenes information came from an article in the *Los Angeles Times* (11/14/2006). The Hittite water-carrier story came from Robert Garland, "Daily Life of the Ancient Greeks" (*Greenwood Daily Life Online*, dailylife.greenwood.com/dle.jsp?k=2&x=10&bc=DBDL1311&p=5-1).

Chapter Four

The ancient Greeks' use of wine to clean wounds comes from Tom Standage's *A History of the World in Six Glasses* (New York: Walker & Company, 2005, page 59).

Chapter Five

Much of the information about the Etruscans, the gods of the sewers, and the gastra comes from Horan, *The Porcelain God* (pages 11, 13, and 17). Information about living in *insulae*, as well as Roman banquets, comes in part from Don Nardo's *Life in Ancient Rome,* The Way People Live series (San Diego: Lucent Books, 1997, pages 45, 69), and also from a great article by Roger D. Hansen about water supply, daily living, and the question of lead poisoning, entitled "Water and Wastewater Systems in Imperial Rome" (online at http://www.waterhistory.org/histories/rome/).

Chapter Six

A great summary of the decline of the Frankish Empire and about the rise of feudalism can be found in Earle Rice Jr.'s *Life During the Middle Ages,* The Way People Live series (San Diego: Lucent Books, 1998, pages 14–15). Descriptions about delousers can be found in Georges Vigarello's *Concepts of Cleanliness: Changing Attitudes in France Since the Middle Ages* (trans. by Jean Birrell; Cambridge: Cambridge University Press, 1988, page 42) as well as the quotation from the fifteenth-century etiquette book (J. Sulpizio as quoted in Vigarello, page 42). Some of the more colorful details about the job of knight's squire come from the entertaining Web site Worst Jobs in History (Tony Robinson, www.channel4.com/history/microsites/W/worstjobs/). Running up the sides of the dung heap comes from Donald Reid's *Paris Sewers and Sewermen* (Cambridge: Harvard University Press, 1991, page 10). Details about barber surgeons from James Wynbrandt, *The Excruciating History of Dentistry* (New York: St. Martin's Press, 1998, page 41), and Liza Picard, *Dr. Johnson's London* (New York: St. Martin's Press, 2000, see chapter 16 on dentistry and medical care). Although the latter book covers a later period (the 1700s), there's a great description of barber surgeons, who hadn't evolved much since medieval times.

Chapter Seven

Jeffrey Singman's *Daily Life in Elizabethan England* (Westport, CT: Greenwood Press, 1995, pages 136–137) has a lot of information about what people drank during the Renaissance, as does William Manchester's *A World Lit Only by Fire: The Medieval Mind and the Renaissance* (Boston: Little, Brown, 1992, page 54). The account of the cocoa beans being burned on the ship is related in *Great Events from History: The Renaissance and Early Modern Era* (Pasadena: Salem Press, 2005, page 522), edited by Christina J. Moose. Liza Picard's *Elizabeth's London: Everyday Life in Elizabethan London* (New York: St. Martin's Press, 2003, pages 133, 144) has great descriptions of what people wore, as does Singman (especially codpieces; see pages 100–101). Horan's *Porcelain God* recounts the story of the Earl of Oxford and has a good summary of Sir John Harington's toilet invention (pages 48–49, 59). What they drank in the New World comes from David F. Hawke's *Everyday Life in Early America* (New York: Harper and Row, 1988, pages 78–80). A very helpful history-of-plumbing Web site includes an account of da Vinci's invention in an article by Maureen Frances, "The Flush Toilet: A Tribute to Ingenuity" (www.masterplumbers.com/plumbviews/1999/toilet_tribute2.asp).

Chapter Eight

Descriptions of the water supply, street signs, traffic, trades, and executions rely on two main sources: Richard B. Schwartz's *Daily Life in Johnson's London* (Madison: University of Wisconsin Press, 1983, pages 13–15, executions 148–151) as well as Liza Picard's *Restoration London* (New York: St. Martin's Press, 1997, pages 7, 9–11). Picard also describes the Pepys/Lady Sandwich anecdote (page 40). Accounts of the dangers of bathing and the anecdote about Henry IV come from Vigarello (pages 11–12). Dictating wills at the top of their lungs is recounted in Vigarello (page 7), and the accounts of Louis XIV's appetite and autopsy from Nancy Mitford, *The Sun King* (New York: Harper and Row, 1993, pages 100, 149) as well as from W. H. Lewis,

The Splendid Century (Garden City, New York: Doubleday and Co., 1957, page 56). The goose-neck anecdote is from Horan (page 145).

Chapter Nine

The description of Venice's concert halls comes from M. Andrieux, *Daily Life in Venice at the Time of Casanova* (trans. by Mary Fitton; London: George Allen and Unwin, 1972, pages 186–187). Japan's and China's sanitation history comes from Susan B. Hanley, "Urban Sanitation in Preindustrial Japan" (*Journal of Interdisciplinary History* 18, no. 1 [Summer 1987], The MIT Press, pages 1–26). The description of the perils of kimonos comes from Horan (page 157). The after-dinner chamber-pot information comes from Schwartz (pages 14–15). The description of how ladies peed while wearing long dresses comes from Frank Muir, *An Irreverent and Almost Complete Social History of the Bathroom* (New York: Stein and Day, 1976, page 114).

Chapter Ten

The statistics about death rate, birth rate, and London's population come from a Web site article by David Cody entitled "A Brief History of London" (http://www.victorianweb.org/history/hist4.html). Accounts of horses and carts getting swallowed up are recounted in an article by Mary Gayman, "A Glimpse into London's Early Sewers" (reprinted from *Cleaner* magazine at www.swopnet.com/engr/londonsewers/londontext3.html). Descriptions of sedan chairs rely on Liza Picard, *Dr. Johnson's London* (New York: St. Martin's Press, 2000, page 26), and Schwartz (page 11). The account of the Fleet explosion is noted by Stephen Halliday, *The Great Stink of London: Sir Joseph Bazalgette and the Cleansing of the Victorian Metropolis* (Phoenix Mill, England: Sutton, 2000, pages 27–28), and from W. Hodding Carter, *Flushed: How the Plumber Saved Civilization* (New York: Atria, 2006, page 109). The tea-drinking trend is recounted by Standage (pages 187–188) and also by Johnson (page 95); much of the information about the gin craze is from Picard's *Dr. Johnson's London* (page 124) and also from Stephen Inwood, *A History of London* (New York: Carroll and Graf, 1998, pages 276–278).

Chapter Eleven

The description of rookeries comes in part from Diane Yancey's excellent book *Life in Charles Dickens's England*, The Way People Live series (San Diego: Lucent Books, 1999, page 45). I also found helpful her fine summary of the origins of the Industrial Revolution (pages 15–16). Descriptions of the poor were aided by Inwood (page 516) and also by Anthony Wohl, *Endangered Lives: Public Health in Victorian Britain* (Cambridge: Harvard University Press, 1983, pages 48, 61–65, 76–79).

Chapter Twelve

The sections about the dangers of flush toilets benefited greatly from Johnson (page 114), and statistics on toilet use in America from Joel Tarr, *The Search for the Ultimate Sink: Urban Pollution in Historical Perspective* (Akron: University of Akron Press, 1996, page 115). Details about water companies and the story of live eels coming through drains come from Liza Picard, *Victorian London: The Life of a City 1840–1870* (New York: St. Martin's Press, 2005, page 64), and more about water companies turning off water from Wohl (page 62) and from http://theplumber.com/plague.html. Information about horses (manure, life expectancy, dead animals) comes from an article written by Joel Tarr and Clay McShane entitled "The Centrality of the Horse to the Nineteenth-Century American City," which is excerpted at www.enviroliteracy.org, and also from Tarr's *Ultimate Sink* (pages 323–324, 327). A description of modern-day rendering plants appears in an article in the *New York Times* (3/11/1997).

Chapter Thirteen

I relied on Steven Johnson's book (*Ghost Map*), with its riveting account of the physical effects of cholera (pages 35–40) and its informative summary of John Snow and the Broad Street pump (pages 144–146). Additional information about cholera comes in part from Wohl (pages 118–125).

Chapter Fourteen

Accounts of Bazalgette and the Big Stink come in part from Picard's *Victorian London* (pages 52–53) and from Johnson (pages 205–210).

Chapter Fifteen

Much of the information in the toilet timeline is summarized by Tarr, *Ultimate Sink* (page 136). Julius Adams information comes from the Web site article "History of Plumbing in America" (from *Plumbing and Mechanical*, July 1987/plumber.com). Some of the Paris Big Stink details come from Donald Reid's *Paris Sewers and Sewermen* (Cambridge: Harvard University Press, 1991, page 81), and also from David S. Barnes, "Confronting Sensory Crisis in the Great Stinks of London and Paris," a chapter in *Filth: Dirt, Disgust and Modern Life* (W. Cohen and R. Johnson, eds., Minneapolis: University of Minnesota Press, 2005, see in particular pages 106–110).

Chapter Sixteen

Some of the information about the history of sanitation in New York, including Waring and Biggs information, can be found in Edwin G. Burrows and Mike Wallace, *Gotham: A History of New York City to 1898* (New York: Oxford University Press, 1999, pages 588, 1194, 1197). The story of President Garfield and the White House sewer problems comes from James Whorton, "'The Insidious Foe'—Sewer Gas" (*Western Journal of Medicine,* www.pubmedcentral.nih.gov/articlerender.fcgi?artid=1275984).

Chapter Seventeen

You can watch astronaut Chris Hadfield recount how astronauts go to the bathroom at this site: http://www.youtube.com/watch?v=HUe2HcFUPSo (among other places on the Web). The toilet mist problem is described in an article by Mary Roach entitled "What I Learned from Dr. Clean" (as quoted in Horan, page 189).

Chapter Eighteen

The story of the alligator in the sewer was reported in the *New York Times* (2/10/1935). Euphemisms for the toilet come from Muir, *An Irreverent and Almost Complete Social History of the Bathroom* (page 146). The history of diapers was helped by a Web site: Disposable Diaper History (www.richernet.com/history.htm) and also by William Rathje and Cullen Murphy, *Rubbish: The Archaeology of Garbage* (New York: HarperCollins, 1992, page 151). The cloth-versus-disposable debate is addressed by Rathje and Murphy (page 162) and also in an article at abcnews.go.com/technology/story?id=789465&page=3. Sewage-powered fuel cells are explained in Carter (pages 221–222). The statistics about toilets in the developing world come from a *New York Times* article (11/14/2006).

Acknowledgments

I owe thanks to a great many people for their support and enthusiasm while I've worked on this book, including my friends and fellow writers Michaela Muntean, Marcia DeSanctis, and Dani Shapiro; Dr. Eric Salk, for his accessibility and patient explanations in response to my naive and misguided questions about germs, viruses, vectors, and fecal-oral diseases; Peter Frew and Yee-Fun Yin for their photographs; Mark and Edie Traina, for loaning me their baby; Ann Leary, for loaning me her horse; Mike Sartori, for answering my innumerable plumbing questions; Loree Griffin Burns, for her advice with image research; Luke and Beth Albee, for their assistance with securing many of the images for the book; all the helpful, knowledgeable librarians at the Taft School Library, for providing me with a pleasant and welcoming de facto office over the course of researching and writing the book, and for ordering dozens of interlibrary loan books for me; my smart, insightful editor, Emily Easton; my diligent and creative design team, Dani Delaney and Donna Mark; Robert Leighton, the hilariously talented cartoonist who gave the book the extra injection of humor that it needed; my congenial and supportive agent, Caryn Wiseman; and to my fellow members of SCBWI.

And thanks most especially to my husband, Jon, and my children, Sam, Cassie, and Luke, who get their own paragraph for putting up with my incessant toilet talk.

Picture Credits

Index

Note: Page numbers in *italics* indicate illustrations.